Sacrifice, Captivity and Escape

For my Beloved wife Aileen,
for whom this memoir was originally written.

Sacrifice, Captivity and Escape

The Remarkable Memoirs of a Japanese POW

PETER JACKSON

Pen & Sword
MILITARY

First published in Great Britain in 2012 by
PEN & SWORD MILITARY
An imprint of
Pen & Sword Books Ltd
47 Church Street
Barnsley
South Yorkshire
S70 2AS

ISBN 978-1-84884-835-1

A CIP catalogue record for this book is available from the British Library

Typeset by Concept, Huddersfield, West Yorkshire
Printed and bound in England by CPI Group (UK) Ltd, Croydon, CRO 4YY

Pen & Sword Books Ltd incorporates the imprints of Pen & Sword Aviation,
Pen & Sword Family History, Pen & Sword Maritime, Pen & Sword Military,
Pen & Sword Discovery, Wharncliffe Local History, Wharncliffe True Crime,
Wharncliffe Transport, Pen & Sword Select, Pen & Sword Military Classics,
Leo Cooper, The Praetorian Press, Remember When, Seaforth Publishing and
Frontline Publishing.

For a complete list of Pen & Sword titles please contact
PEN & SWORD BOOKS LIMITED
47 Church Street, Barnsley, South Yorkshire, S70 2AS, England
E-mail: enquiries@pen-and-sword.co.uk
Website: www.pen-and-sword.co.uk

Contents

Foreword

This is an incredible story of one citizen soldier during the Second World War. Britain was battling for its survival and the young, recently married Peter Jackson was conscripted into the British Army. He spent his first year in training and in defending Britain against the potential German invasion. His war really starts when his regiment is posted to the Far East and he finds himself on Singapore Island, just before the final Japanese assault and ignominious surrender. Like all soldiers he has no idea what is happening beyond his immediate horizon. He finds himself a prisoner of the Japanese and luck and happening to have the right skills allows him to survive a year of captivity on the island before being sent north to work on the 'Death Railway' in Thailand. Here cholera, malaria, dysentery, starvation rations, the deliberate brutality and casual neglect by Japanese guards leads to thousands of deaths.

Jackson finds himself in a cholera camp. The chance discoveries of a map and compass and an unguarded rice store, leads to an improbable escape with no certainty of where they are heading. Their aim is to travel through Burma towards China. Death on-the-run seems preferable to the inevitable death sentence facing them in camp. But while escaping they suffer hunger, tiredness, and sickness. All but one survives and they spend the monsoon sheltering in a limestone cave. Betrayed by the villagers the surviving men find themselves facing life sentences in the infamous Outram Road Jail on Singapore Island.

When Peter is ill with beriberi he is sent to Changi to die, but he lives thanks to the care he receives in the Changi Prison hospital. He becomes one of the living dead, whose death is faked, to keep him from being sent back to Outram Road and he lives and survives in Changi by his wits.

It is a story simply told where chance and happenstance determine Jackson's fate. Yet it is gripping in its simplicity because he and his comrades do the impossible, escaping from the Japanese, surviving the rigors of that escape and then even more improbably surviving recapture.

Peter Jackson, now in his nineties, wrote this for his second wife, Aileen, and we are lucky that he did so. If this was a novel it would be dismissed as being too implausible. Jackson lays no claim to leadership nor does he give deep insights into his personal suffering, but it still resonates through what he does not say. Although written in his old age, this is a young man's story of a war without heroes, one of chaos and muddle, horror and endurance, and most of all of surviving in the face of impossible odds. It is a book to read and ponder upon.

Christopher Pugsley
Department of War Studies
Royal Military Academy Sandhurst

Chapter 1

Childhood

There have been many books written about, and by, admirals, adjutants and athletes, by generals and Germans right through the alphabet to politicians and zealots, but there have been few books written by me. I am one of the millions of nobodies whom generals and admirals found to be expendable in wartime. They were able to move us hither and thither as though we were nothing more nor less than pawns in a game of chess. I was one of those men of whom the general said, 'We must sacrifice that platoon, or company or brigade', after they had made some stupid blunder.

I am one of the thousands to whom politicians speak, and about, when they want me to vote for them; one of those who sit back and let it all happen, yet are still able to think and act for ourselves and yet have no power to alter the course of history.

Who am I? Let me call myself a pawn in the game of life. My story starts the day I was born, 4 January 1919. My life span runs from the horse and cart era through the first motor cars to landing a man on the moon, to super computers.

I was one of those unlucky blighters who was used and regarded as dispensable in the Second World War. I was conscripted into the army soon after the war started; I was only twenty years old and had just married. After serving in Britain I was shipped off to India and then to Singapore. I arrived only a few weeks before the city fell to the Japanese. I then spent nearly four years as a prisoner of the Imperial Japanese government. I survived fortuitously and am now, at the time of writing, ninety-two. This is my story of those years.

I was born in London in Queen Charlotte's Hospital. It appears that they didn't think much of me. They put drops of brandy in my feed to pep me up and I was thin and ugly. My mother said a nurse told her, 'ugly in the cradle but pretty at the table'. Most of my early memories are of frugal living. My mother and father did their best to

1

provide for me but life was a hard struggle for them. I know that at times they went without in order to feed me.

My father served in the 1914–1918 war in the Royal Artillery. His feet were a mess from frostbite. A gun carriage had run over his toes so, at times, it was difficult for him to walk. He had also been deafened by the sound of gunfire. It appears that none of this war service entitled him to a pension. Before the war he had spent time in the navy so he had scars on his back from where he was beaten. He was able to show me a windjammer and name every sail, spar and piece of rigging and equipment on it. None of this equipped him for civilian life. I remember him as a builder's labourer with hard callused hands that were often cracked and sore. Although frequently unemployed he was somehow able to get a little money. For a while he worked in the rubber trade, but a crash in its price put him out of a job. Back then many children didn't know what their dads did. Their fathers came home at night, tired and dirty and not likely to say much about what they had done. He got the dole but it was a mere pittance. I can remember on more than one occasion my mother and father were given a Christmas food parcel so that we could have some sort of celebration.

My mother also worked but she never complained. She did housework for someone else who, we used to say, 'had a position to keep up'. Each day she would take me to a woman who looked after me while she went to work. The lady was very kind but was sick a lot. Someone was always looking for a bottle of soda water and one day I heard the doctor say she had dropsy. Her name was Mrs Warboys and she used to wash my face and hands and sit me in a high backed armchair so that I was clean when my mother came to pick me up – sometimes I was there for hours.

I started school at five years old and went into the infants' class. It cost two shillings and sixpence per week for me to have a dinner. The senior girls did the cooking as part of their education. How my mother managed to pay that amount I shall never know. Each child was served and grace was said before we started to eat. We were always admonished to eat up as our parents had paid good money for the food. Miss Saxford, a rather large imposing woman, dressed in spotless white, had a cane nearby. She used it on the odd occasion when something was served up we didn't like. Miss Saxford yelled, 'You will eat up all your dinner,' WHACK on the desk. 'You will not leave here until you have eaten every morsel,' WHACK on the desk.

2

'Look, Jackson has eaten all of his pease pudding,' (which I liked). I always ate it up because I knew that if there was some left over Madam would offer me a little more. Mind you, it was always a bit windy where I sat in the afternoon!

I also remember Miss Jones with brown brogue shoes, tweed skirts, woollen jumpers (winter and summer), with her hair always pulled tight back with a bun on each ear. She was known as 'Earphone Annie'. We dared not even whisper that name though, as there was always the cane hanging on the edge of the blackboard. She was not allowed to cane us. She had to get a master to come and do it. We kids knew it was only because she couldn't hit us hard enough.

One teacher we really liked was Mr Warren. He was the English master and very good at teaching poetry. Robert Louis Stevenson's 'Revenge' was one of my favourites. The start of the poem was soft and gentle:

'Twas at Flores in the Azores where Sir Richard Grenville lay,
When a pinnace like a fluttered bird came flying from far away,
Spanish ships of war at sea, we have sighted fifty-three.

Then, on into the middle of the battle he would go, his voice rising with excitement and fingers pointing:

Ship after ship the whole night long,
Through the battle thunders and flame,
Ship after ship the whole night long,
Went down in the Spanish Maine.

He left me with a love of poetry and geography. Whereas other teachers unrolled a map on the wall, he would bring his magic lantern, the forerunner of the slide projector, to class and show us views of cities and countries.

If we got into trouble outside of school, what school we attended was discovered and the school could punish us.

My mother instilled a sense of pride into me. She attended our local high church and I went both to church and Sunday school. At mass I was an altar boy. I sang in the choir. I belonged to Wolf Cubs and Boy Scouts as I got older. All these activities have stood me in good stead.

Our home was quite near Hampstead Heath and Parliament Hill. Both were within easy walking distance. They covered a large area of land and had three or four ponds. The fishing pond was one I never bothered with as I had no time for standing doing nothing – that was for older men. The model boat pond, however, my dad and I used. I, like him, was good with my hands and I had made a good sized model yacht at woodwork. Dad, being an ex-sailor, made the sails and rigging for it and we had some good fun sailing it. The other pond that I used, in company with hundreds of others, was the swimming pond.

We had a lot of fun in winter as snow on Parliament Hill meant we could go sledging – tobogganing was not a word we used then. When the snow became packed hard like ice we went at great speeds, little realizing it was so dangerous. One day I had a great idea. 'How about we all go down together on the sledge,' I suggested. We arranged it so that I was leader. I lay flat on my stomach with the three girls sitting on my back and the two boys sitting on and between my splayed legs. We managed to settle ourselves fairly comfortably and away we went down the hill, gathering speed as we went. The girls screamed and the boys shouted and laughed. Suddenly, the sledged lurched to the left. I tried to control it but it was impossible. I was face down on the sledge with five others on top of me. In front of us was a large tree and near that a pile of gravel. I steered the sledge towards the gravel. We were all got thrown off and I shot forward off the sledge into the gravel. I was lucky to only graze my head but my parents got a shock when I arrived home.

One pond was very shallow and was considered safe for ice skating or just larking about on. Not many of us kids could afford ice skates but we used to have a lot of fun making long slides on the ice. The pond was shallow, so if you went through the thin ice you only got your legs and feet wet.

One day I got a penny and decided to buy some chips at the fried fish shop. I remember going into the shop and getting my chips. The next thing I knew I was waking up in a hospital with my head bandaged. I had walked out of the shop and been hit by an on-coming car as I crossed the road.

I had another stay in hospital at thirteen. I fell ill with bad stomach pains. Mum called the doctor and he diagnosed acute appendicitis. For the first time in my life I was driven in a taxi cab to the hospital. I was immediately operated on and afterwards told that peritonitis had set in so the operation was urgent.

There was one bully-boy who took a dislike to me and was always calling me names. Back then my family had no money for footwear. The school had a storeroom and parents donated children's used clothing to the school for people like me. When I needed shoes, the only ones left were a pair of button-up girl's boots. I was horrified. Only the bully-boy made something of it. He called me, 'Old Girlie Jackson,' and it wasn't long before other kids took up the chant. Suddenly, I lost my temper and we were fighting. It was only when I banged his head on the ground that we stopped. After that we became good friends and never fought again.

Academically, my performance was poor. Arithmetic was my worst subject and mental arithmetic, as it was called, was a nightmare. Questions such as, 'If one-and-a-half sweets cost one-and-a-half pence, how much would five sweets cost?' All the clever kids' hands would go up, as would mine, but I was desperately hoping the teacher wouldn't ask me to answer. Of course, he did, because he knew my answer would be wrong and it was good for a laugh. I had no trouble with writing and spelling. I was reasonably good at geography, very good at woodwork, metalwork and basket weaving. At twelve years old I made my own crystal wireless set.

The mention of geography brings to mind the thought of a big map that hung on the wall in every classroom. It was a map of the whole world and on it were all the countries of the British Empire marked in red. We children were taught to be very patriotic. The Empire was our heritage and we were expected to guard it well.

Each year we celebrated Empire Day, which we really looked forward to. The big attraction was the school pageant. This was a history of England as a parade and we were dressed as a character from some part of English history. Queen Boadicea was the favourite. I served once as a Roman soldier, and another time as a Viking. I would have loved to have been a Crusader in armour, but missed out.

Days before the pageant, the teachers and we children would be cutting up cardboard and crepe paper and Mums would be sewing at home. In fact, it was nearly as exciting as Christmas. We sang songs such as *Land of Hope and Glory*, *Jerusalem*, and *Onward Christian Soldiers*, and had lots of other martial music. We were all very proud to play our part for our great Empire.

The school leaving age at that time was fourteen, at which age the majority of the poorer kids left. My mother had mentioned to a friend that I was due to leave school shortly and heard there was a vacancy for a junior messenger at the Railway Clearing House. On my fourteenth birthday I was given my first pair of long trousers. My school results had been good enough for me to continue my education free of charge at our local Polytechnical College. However, my father had other ideas and said, 'If you think you're going to school now you're in long trousers, you're wrong. It's out to work for you my lad.'

Chapter 2

Downstairs

On 12 April 1933 I attended an interview and a medical examination at the Railway Clearing House at Euston to see whether I was fit to be employed as a temporary junior messenger. After the interview and medical examination were over I was told that there were other applicants for the job and I would be notified of the results by post.

I was surprised to receive a letter a few days later:

Sir,

Referring to your call here yesterday, we shall have a vacancy for a junior messenger on Monday, 1st of May and if you are prepared to accept this position you must attend here to take up your duties at 9.00am on that date.

The conditions of service have already been explained to you and you will receive a wage of 15s 7d per week (16s 0d less 2½% National Wages Board deduction).

Yours obediently

P. H. Price

A letter also arrived telling me to report to the tailor to be measured for a uniform which, when made, I collected before starting work. The uniform was made of black serge and consisted of two pairs of trousers, one long-sleeved waistcoat and one single-breasted jacket, with chromium-plated silver buttons. Added to this were two pairs of black woollen socks and one pair of boots. Each year we were issued with a new outfit. I had to supply a white semi-stiff collar and a tie, which were to be worn at all times. My mother and father were overjoyed to think that not only was I going to earn money, but they were not going to have to spend money on my clothing. But I hated the uniform. It was so stiff and new that it felt like a suit of armour.

7

On 1 May 1933 I duly reported to the head messenger and was taken downstairs to a dark, dingy basement. The office I was shown into was Dickensian. It was a large, artificially lit room, with a big steel-covered table in it. All round the walls were racks and racks of bundles of paper tied up with string. Off this room were what looked like tunnels lined with more and more racks of dusty bundles. It was our job to find the files the clerks upstairs requested. The first thing we did was to pick up a hand held electric lamp with about five yards of flex. We then went to the tunnel where the required bundle was housed. Each rack held many bundles, all covered in thick dust. When the correct bundles were found, my co-worker Bud would disappear with them on a barrow. At other times a clerk would come down from the upstairs offices and ask in person for a special bundle, then wait for us to find them. They would open the bundle on the metal topped table and start to make notes of the contents. Staff liked to come down to our department in the winter. Each upstairs office held about a hundred men and the only form of heating was by a coal fire on one side of the room. Our department was heated the same way but was a very small area and was always lovely and warm. The clerks would stand with their backs to the fire and browse through their bundle of paper.

My boss was Mr Dobbin, always referred to as Old Dobby. He introduced me to the other staff. A man called Bud was much older than I and another boy, perhaps sixteen or seventeen, was called Titch. Being the new boy was hard going. I was called on to go to the oldest and dirtiest parts. However, I made the best of it and Bud and Titch treated me well.

At first I found Titch very disconcerting. He was always going around shadow boxing or punching at anything that was soft enough. He was small but fit and nimble and, according to Bud, was able to make money as a lightweight boxer. As we got to know each other better, we would often spar. Titch was a real cockney kid and would dance around me saying, 'Come on, 'ave a go, try an' 'it me.' I did try to hit him but he was too fast for me. Bud was on the permanent staff and was classed as a senior messenger.

The room in which we worked had a gallery around it, about eight feet above us. This was surrounded by a guard rail with three bars one above the other. The balcony was reached by a ladder which I used until I caught up with Titch and Bud. When anything was wanted from the gallery the race was on. They didn't bother with the ladder. For them it was a jump up, grabbing the edge of the balcony and then climb one, two, three, hand-over-hand up the bars and a roll over the top on to the balcony floor. There they would grab the bundle and chuck it down onto the table. The losers had to give the winner a cigarette. As I was always last I got fed up with giving away cigarettes I could ill-afford, so when no-one was around I started to exercise and soon was able to compete with them. After I won a couple of times it was decided to discontinue the game.

After a year down in the dungeons I had grown out of my uniform and it was time for a new one and so I went off to the tailor to be measured. The clean white collars cost nine pence-halfpenny each and two pence each for laundering, which it was my responsibility to pay. I was told not to go down into the dungeon but to go up to the third floor and report to Mr Mumford in 'A Division'. I don't think I slept much that night. I was filled with anticipation and fear for what awaited me that next day.

Mr Mumford was sitting at his desk and I duly introduced myself. He showed me to a chair on the other side of his desk and produced some papers on which were all my instructions and timetables. He told me to study them and memorize all I could. I was to work in 'A Division' as messenger for four offices, each one containing 100 men. I was to climb the stairs hundreds of times from that day on. There was a lift but it was of an antiquated design. Junior staff were not allowed to use it because it was thought to be dangerous.

Employees working for the railway had many benefits, such as low cost travel and a certain number of free passes per year. One of my numerous duties was the issuing of Privilege Ticket (PT) forms to members of the staff. Each morning I had to go through the office enquiring if anybody wanted one. It allowed us to buy tickets at one-quarter the full fare. Although only a junior member of the staff I was entitled to PTs and also one free pass per year. As it was necessary for me to travel to work by Underground I was able to get a quarter rate season ticket, which lasted for three months. There were no restrictions on its use. One could use it ten times a day if necessary.

It was my responsibility to organize tea for the men, but the method was archaic. Each office had a large water jug and a teapot. At 2.55 I started the tea round. I collected a jug and a pot from the first office, took it down into the basement where the staff kept

9

several large kettles of water boiling on open fires. The jug was filled with tea from one of the large pots. I carried it up the six flights of stairs to the office and then repeated the procedure another three times. Inevitably, one day I tripped on a stair and boiling tea spilt all over my right leg and foot. I passed out and was on crutches for some time. After that all junior staff were forbidden to make the tea. The men took it in turns to do it and were able to use the lift. The men were very good to me. They had made a collection for me and on my return to work presented me with about three pounds – a lot of money at that time.

Each year the staff had an annual outing. I was always included in these occasions and the men made a collection of loose change for me the day before the outing. It was usually enough to give me a good time at fun fairs. The first outing I remember was to Southend-on-Sea. When we arrived at Southend it was a real English seaside morning – cold, wet and miserable. The men disappeared in groups into each pub we passed. I was told to be at a certain hotel on time for midday dinner. I turned up and had my first experience of dining in a really high class restaurant. The man I sat next to guided me as to what cutlery I should use.

My final memory was of a river cruise on the River Thames to Kew Gardens. For the men it was a chance to drink. I did not drink alcohol so was quite content to sit in the sun and watch the scenery drift by; a really lovely day out all in all.

I had a privilege ticket to travel anywhere in the United Kingdom once a year. It was used by family men at holiday time to take their family as far as it was possible to travel. My own journeys were to Aldeburgh to camp with a friend where we met two German girls for a week. Looking back, we thought that as Aldeburgh is on the east coast of England they were probably spying, because no-one in their right mind would want to spend a holiday in Aldeburgh.

Another trip took me to the Kyle of Lochalsh in Scotland. There is a path that skirts the cliffs above the bay. Mrs Shearer, whom I stayed with, suggested that as she was going out for the day, would I like some sandwiches and to walk the cliff path to pass the day, as it took about five hours?

I left the cottage in the morning and slowly wended my way up the path to the top of the cliffs. It was a superb view and one could see right across to the Isle of Skye and even see the ferry boat crossing back and forth. I had no watch so time really had no relevance for me. I thought it must be about lunch time when it started to get misty and very soon it turned to a fog. Of course, I had not realized it but the height of the path had reached low cloud level. I came to a bend in the path and sat on a rock to eat my lunch. Afterwards I leaned back against the bank and dozed off to sleep. The next thing I was waking up with the hot sun on my face and there, ahead of me, was another cliff. At the very point at which I had stopped for lunch the path took a sudden left-hand turn. One more step and I would have gone straight down onto the rocks below. I never did finish the cliff path walk but went back the way I had come feeling quite shaken.

Chapter 3

Home Life

The 1930s were a time of political awareness. A vast number of men were unemployed and, at the same time, we had the threat of Nazism and Fascism hanging over us. I met someone who introduced me to the Young Communist League, whose headquarters were in Mornington Crescent. My father was one of a great pool of unemployed and an ex-war veteran, and I was working for a capitalist organization like the Railways. This made me an ideal candidate for Leninism and Marxism. I soaked up Communism like a sponge. No longer would I be a Boy Scout. My Boy Scout's shirt soon had a red hammer and sickle on each sleeve. My red Boy Scout's scarf became my red flag for marches. I stopped going to church – it was only a sop for a capitalist society.

I was nearly eighteen and at the Railway Clearing House I would either be sacked or given a permanent job. I was quite sure I would be sacked because I had committed some indiscretions. For one thing, I took full advantage of my sick leave – not a good idea in those days. In the morning there was a rush to beat the start work bell, and I was not always successful. Uniform was to be worn at all times but I would disappear about 4.30pm and change into sports coat and flannels. I did this because I had fallen in love with a girl who worked in the typing pool. I walked her to her train and made a date with her. Her father or mother got to know of my interest in their daughter and I was summoned to the office of the Head of Department. Liaisons between staff were not looked on favourably, particularly between the uniformed staff and the clerical staff, so this was another black mark. We still saw each other for a time but it was such a hole-in-the-corner affair that we gradually parted company.

Instead of staying, I got a job as a joiner with a firm of shop fitters. Getting to work was a real problem. I could not afford a bus or train so I had to cycle. I rode fifteen miles a day, six days a week through central London. The thing that I remember was the hunger. I always felt hungry. One of my early jobs in the factory was to run errands for the men: go to the cake shop, for instance. I would buy several cream or fancy cakes in the bakery. The smell was tantalizing but I had no money even to buy one cake for myself.

The men in the shop-fitters factory were a totally different type to the men at the Railway Clearing House. There were no tips when I helped them. I found they had coarse language and, at times, felt contempt for them. Perhaps it was just as well that this interlude in my life lasted less than a year. The one bright spot was working in a store at Watford. A well-known chain store had set the date for a grand opening and to meet this deadline it became necessary to work overtime. The hours were something like 7.30am to 10.00pm for three or four days, with a final burst of twenty-four hours over a weekend. That week I earned more money than I ever had in my life. Two weeks later I became unemployed as the firm went bankrupt.

After leaving the job at Croydon I thought it was time for a break from working so I was in no hurry to seek another job. But, whilst out walking, I passed a factory quite near to my home and saw a notice saying 'Machinist Wanted'. I had worked on machines at the shop fitters and so applied for the job. After explaining that my previous employer had gone bankrupt and telling of my experience as a tradesman, I got the job.

I was not yet nineteen, nor was I a qualified tradesman, but that didn't prevent the firm from using me on skilled work. The firm went under the name of 'The Display Construction Company' and, as its name implies, specialized in shop display units. As I had already worked as a shop fitter the work was very similar. One day I cut through the top of my thumb and when I returned to work I was told my services were no longer needed.

A friend of my mother's was instrumental in finding my next job – delivering groceries. The first few weeks were like a holiday. I could walk to work and if it rained I was supplied with wet weather gear. Also, anything my mother or I bought was always a little cheaper. Ham bones always had a nice bit of ham left on them, bacon ends were, at times, half rashers of bacon, and damaged tins of fruit that just had a dent in them were often very cheap to buy.

During the time that I was delivering, the customers got to know me and some of the older ladies would ask me in for a cup of tea, particularly if the weather was wet. I would have to refuse and I was given a small tip instead. Most people ran an account but there were the odd cash customers; they were the ones I liked. If the bill was, for instance, £1 11s 10d there was always two pence in it for me because I had no change. Sometimes I would collect, maybe, a shilling in one day. That was extra to my pay and was MY MONEY!

Christmas came and there were mountains of orders for hams, turkeys and chickens. On 23 December the whole staff sat down after the shop closed at nine o'clock and we were given a huge meal. At 9.30pm we started plucking fresh chickens, turkeys and geese. We plucked all night and the shop opened at the usual time the next morning for business. I was on my bike and away with the orders for nearly twelve hours. I went home that Christmas Eve with an extra ten bob in my pay, a bottle of port wine and a freshly plucked chicken. We had a great Christmas.

I wanted to return to my trade and I had no trouble getting another job quite near home. It was in a cabinet-making factory and the job was quite easy after the grocery business. By then there was talk of war. I had only been at this firm for a short time when a rumour circulated that the government was going to start conscription. The rumour soon became a reality and I was ordered to report to a place in Hendon, London, for a medical check-up prior to being conscripted into the Army.

Unfortunately, at this time the government had informed employers that any man who was called up must have his job kept open for him regardless of how long he was in the Army. I went to have my medical test and was pronounced A1, fit for active service. Next day at work I went to the machine and it was all cleaned and dusted down; the pile of wood had also disappeared. Then the foreman came over and said, 'You must come with me to the office.' It seemed that the wood I had cut the day before going for my medical had all been cut the wrong size. Added to that, the master cutting list that had the sizes on it had disappeared. Therefore, they had no alternative other than to dismiss me. No use protesting, certainly no use calling them liars, and so I was out of a job once again. I later learnt this was a common practice.

I got a job at Heathmans Ladder Works at Parsons Green as a sawmill worker. The money was good but the hours were long.

14

Heathmans made all kinds of ladders from small household steps to fire escapes, for engines, turntables, water towers. The big order that they had when I arrived was for 8,000 hook ladders.

Apart from the fact that it was hard work, I did enjoy the job. The men were friendly and did not seem so coarse in speech and manner. I heard that there was a labouring job available and I knew my father could do it even though he was deaf. That evening I couldn't get home fast enough to tell my Dad. Mum, of course, had our tea ready and we sat down at the table together. After a few mouthfuls of food I couldn't contain myself any longer. I said, 'Dad, I think there may be a job for you where I work.'

A moment's silence and Dad said, 'What did you say?'

Then Mum piped up, 'He said that there might be a job for you where he works.'

Well, Dad wanted to know all about it but all I could tell him was that it was a labouring job. Next morning Dad was dressed up, his boots were polished and he was ready to go. I introduced him,

'Bill, this is the man I said was looking for a job. He's my Dad.'

Bill said I should have told him it was my Dad. My father walked rather awkwardly owing to his army injuries and Bill asked him what was wrong with his feet. Dad explained about the gun carriage and frostbite. Bill's only comment was, 'You poor bugger, but you can walk all right, can't you?'

Dad agreed that he could walk all right and that was something I could vouch for. My father could walk for miles and never seem to tire.

This short interview took place in the workshop with several staff members listening. To an outsider it would have sounded as though two men were having a dreadful argument. But, no, it was only two deaf people having a normal conversation.

My dad got the job of labourer and it was the beginning of a new life for him and, in a way, for me as well. For one thing, we travelled together so he made sure I was up in the morning. Eventually, I gather, he was able to do less labouring and became a packer, responsible for the dispatching of the products.

I was quite happy working at the ladder works. Again, I had requested and received a couple of rises in my pay. In those days if you didn't ask, you didn't get a rise. Sometimes, if you did ask you got the sack instead, so it was a bit of a risky business.

Adolf Hitler and Mussolini were on the rampage. Everyone knew that war was coming. We could all see that appeasement would only make these 'monsters' hungrier. Many of us could see what was going to happen, but many of us did the ostrich trick and buried our head in the sawdust, until one day it was pulled out with a big jerk.

I have mentioned before that although not into sports, I was able to bike or walk for miles. Every evening was spent walking or biking. One evening I learnt there was more to life than work and exercise. I had decided that it was time to go home after being out for an evening and so bought a ticket at Goodge Street Underground station to take me to Kentish Town where I lived. I was standing on the platform waiting for a train when a young lady came up to me and said, 'Did you drop this?' and handed my glove to me. I thanked her and probably that would have been the end of the matter but she had a black Scottish terrier on a lead. I've always been an animal lover and made a fuss of the dog while we chatted. I let my train go by. I asked her where she was going. She said, 'Nowhere. I was just taking the dog for a walk when I saw you drop your glove.' I realised that to give me the glove she had purchased a penny ticket to get into the station, so I was in her debt.

The dog belonged to the people for whom she worked. She was a live-in housemaid only five minutes from the station. I never caught the next train either because I walked her home to Gordon Mansions, a block of expensive flats off Tottenham Court Road. We soon went out together and her employers wanted to meet me. I expect they felt some responsibility towards her as a live-in housemaid. Her mother was dead and her father had little interest in her.

My first meeting with her employer was in the end very casual. I called to see her on my way home from work. I went to the back door at the basement where the tradesmen came. A lady answered the door and I asked to speak to Margaret. She said, 'Are you Peter?' She then called out, 'Margaret, Peter's here.' Margaret came rushing through, looking embarrassed; I was feeling uncomfortable. Mrs N looked me up and down and said, 'Oh well, I'll leave you to chat.'

A few minutes later Mr N came in to ask for a corkscrew. It was obvious he had only come in to give me the once-over. I was just about to leave when he came again and asked if I would like a glass of wine or beer. I thanked him politely but refused. At that stage of my life I didn't drink anything like that.

My meetings with Margaret were not on a regular basis. She had only one half day off each week. Most evenings were free after the evening meal, the washing up and walking the dog. By then I was often too tired to go out so it was largely a hit-and-miss romance. I called on her one day and Margaret called me in. Mrs N appeared and said that she was having a big party and she wondered if I would like to help Margaret with clearing tables and washing up. This was a surprise but I agreed.

This proved to be the beginning of my spending more time at their apartment. I don't know whether it was because they liked me, or if I was a source of cheap labour. I didn't get paid but I was well fed and it enabled me to spend many more comfortable hours with Margaret.

Mrs N. had a baby and she had made an arrangement with Margaret to take the baby out in the pram in the afternoon. Usually she walked in Regent's Park, which was quite close by. On Saturdays and Sundays I would meet Margaret and be allowed to go back to the house for tea and to spend the evening with her. They were great people and Margaret's wage was very generous. All her daily living requirements were met, even to toilet soap and talcum powder, and she received one pound a week. I was only getting two pounds per week and was giving some to my mother. I also had food to buy and other expenses. By general standards, she was well off but was dissatisfied.

Mr N was in the Territorial Army and, when in company of other men, was frequently referred to as 'Captain'. I found out the reason for this form of address when he approached me one day and enquired if I had any wish to become a Territorial soldier. He explained that he was a Territorial Captain in a Guards' regiment and he would recommend me to other branches of the army. I explained to him that I had already had my examinations to be drafted into the army and in the event of war would probably be one of the first to be called up. His only comment was, 'Oh, good man, if you want any advice I'll be able to help,' and it was never mentioned again.

Eventually, Margaret upset her employers and she lost her job. This was a real disaster. I helped her to find a bedsit and a job but the money was not enough to pay the rent and buy food, so I helped her out as best I could. My mother and father did not like her very much. As they put it, 'She thinks too much of herself. After all, she's only a housemaid.' My mother was quite upset when she found out that I was helping her with her living expenses. Later I helped her get another live-in job as a housemaid.

I was not particularly keen on meeting Margaret's father, although he wanted to meet me. I was told that he liked his beer and, apparently, in his younger days he had been rather a truculent character. I was worried about the fact he had been a military policeman in the First World War. My dad had told me bad things about the MPs. He was a rather short, thickset man, grey haired and with one eye that looked inflamed. He explained that his eye had been damaged by mustard gas during the war.

He invited Margaret and I to go down to the nearest pub for a few beers but I quickly explained that neither of us drank in pubs. Margaret later told me that he admired me for not being a boozer. The funny thing was that whenever I met him he always tried to get me into a pub for a drink.

During the time I was courting Margaret we parted a couple of times for various reasons, but eventually we came back together. Until we married our sex life was limited to playing about with each other. I had my own room at home but somehow my mum was always able to find an excuse to knock on the door. Neither of us wanted to be caught 'doing things', as we used to say in those days.

As the days went by, it became more and more apparent that war was imminent and I knew that sooner or later I was going to be called up into the army. On that basis, Margaret and I decided to get married, much against my parents' wishes. I told Dad that Margaret was a good cook. He said, 'Look son, you can get a good feed anywhere but what's she like in bed, that's what you want to know.'

Margaret and I carefully read the adverts for flats to let and we saw one that was less than five minutes walk from where I was living with Mum and Dad. I duly went round and saw the landlady and she showed the flat to me. The house consisted of a basement, first, second and third floors, and then an attic flat in the roof. The attic flat was to let at ten shillings per week, the usual going rate. One room was set aside as a bedroom and was adequate to take a double bed and one or two small pieces of furniture. The second room was the living-room where we did everything except sleep. In fact, this was better than many flats, which were little more than one room. There was a large landing at the top of the stairs which had been made into a kitchen and had a gas stove fitted – an unusual bonus in those days. To get to the flat meant climbing four flights of stairs. As a young and fit twenty-one-year-old this presented no problems to me.

In my enthusiasm I parted with five shillings as a deposit to hold the flat until Margaret could come and inspect it. She was not enthusiastic. She was a big girl and not impressed by having to walk up all the stairs. She liked the separate bedroom and the gas stove but asked about the lavatory and bathroom. The landlady then took us down two flights of stairs and showed us a shared lavatory and bathroom. To me this was a point in the flat's favour as a lot of older houses in those days had no bathroom at all and one had to go to the public baths. The house in which I was brought up had a bathroom but this was used only by the landlady and her family. The bathroom door was always kept locked against intruders.

After some discussion between ourselves, Margaret came to the conclusion that marrying me outweighed the disadvantages of having to climb a few stairs and share a bathroom. After all, she would be able to stay home all day and bathe any time she wished as she fully intended to give up work when we married.

All this took place about three weeks before the wedding and so it meant that the rent had to be paid although we were not living in the flat. On the other hand, it enabled us to get ready for moving in after the wedding.

In my spare time I made several items of furniture. There was a kitchen cabinet, which was not only cupboards and drawers but also incorporated a folding table which one could work on when cooking. Also a pair of bedside cabinets made of oak, a coffee table of oak, a small table which would be useful for a radio or a vase of flowers, a fire screen, and a mahogany bureau. This last item was made from a counter top that had been in a chemist's shop that was demolished. It had been brought home by my father on a borrowed barrow. When I told him that the counter top was solid mahogany he said, 'Blimey, I should have brought the other bit but it was too heavy.'

I spent time moving in the furniture that I had made. The kitchen cabinet was made in three sections so that I could move it one section at a time. Some time before this, when I had proposed to Margaret, I had seen a very nice forty-two piece china service that was four pounds. I had paid it off on lay-by and that was my wedding gift. The other furniture that we got on hire purchase was a double bed and a dining table and chairs. By the time we got married the flat was more or less ready to live in.

We had decided on a church wedding and Saturday, 2 September 1939 came around. But in the preceding week all hell had broken loose. War was imminent and we were more or less on a war footing. After the service we walked back to our flat for a small gathering. Margaret's auntie and her companion had journeyed down to London from Manchester with a lovely wedding cake that they had made. They left us at about 7.00pm to go back to Manchester as they were both very nervous about the war situation. By 10.00pm everyone had gone and we were left on our own to face our first night together.

Chapter 4

Called Up

The next morning, Sunday, 3 September 1939, was fine and calm. Margaret had just cooked bacon and eggs when the lady who lived below us asked if we had a radio then said we had better come and listen to hers as there was going to be a very important announcement. Downstairs we heard Neville Chamberlain announce that Britain had declared war on Germany – it was no surprise to us. Then the air raid sirens started to wail; so we headed for the basement. Eventually the 'all clear' went and life returned to normal.

The firm I worked for was making thousands of ladders and other rescue equipment for the government. I hoped that as the firm was on war work I would be exempt from the army. I arrived home one evening to find Margaret with a very sad face. She had opened a letter addressed to me. She said she could not go through the whole day worrying what the War Department wanted. It was my call-up. On 16 October 1939 I was to report to barracks in Bury St Edmunds to join the Suffolk Regiment. I saw my boss the following day and he told me that no-one under twenty-one was exempt. My birthday was not until January.

Margaret and I tried to carry on our normal life: we went to the pictures, visited our parents, I carried on working and Margaret got a housework job that brought in a little extra money.

Finally I had to catch the train to Bury St Edmunds. Mum, Dad and Margaret came to see me off. Then things became a blur. I remember arriving at Bury St Edmunds station and seeing a soldier standing by a notice board where all new recruits gathered. The soldier gave the order to fall in and follow him. We straggled along the street behind him.

We walked through the gates of the barracks and were told to give our names and addresses to a soldier sitting at a table. Then we were given a large canvas sack and were told to go to a building nearby

21

and fill it with straw. I hadn't got a clue what this was for. As we passed out the other end another soldier issued us with three boards about 6ft long and 8in wide. He said, 'You'll get the trestles later. You lot will bed down in number seventeen platoon hut.'

I had stuffed my bag far too full, so had to make another trip back to the storage hut to empty some straw out. I remember lying on the floor on a pile of straw, wrapped in blankets that felt like sackcloth, crying myself to sleep. I was not the stuff that heroes are made of. I can't even recall having anything to eat or drink. I do know I smoked a whole packet of cigarettes because, when I woke up the next morning, my packet was empty.

The following day we were supposed to be kitted out with army gear. What a shambles; there were boots for some and not others, trousers that didn't match jackets, shirts that were far too big with collars that were far too small. The humour of it all knocked off one or two rough edges.

We were in Bury St Edmunds Barracks for eight weeks of intensive training. No one was allowed to leave the town precincts and no home passes would be issued except on the most compassionate grounds. This came as a shock to young married men.

Each day that passed saw us become more accustomed to army life. Several men were caught by the red-caps (Military Police) trying to get home at weekends. Some, who were lucky enough to be well off, were able to bring their wife to stay with them and get a sleeping-out pass. For me that was impossible. The basic pay for a private soldier was two shillings a day, for a single man. Actually, for a single man this was quite good pay. Most young men seemed to enjoy their cigarettes and beer and movies in the town at the army canteens. For us married men it was a different story. The government took seven shillings a week from our pay to help make up our wives' income, so mine was half of what most of the others were getting. Cigarettes became a luxury. Luckily I didn't drink alcohol so what little money I had went on tea and biscuits at the NAAFI.

After Christmas 1939, when we had finished our initial training, a new intake was due to take over our barracks accommodation. I remained in No. 17 platoon and about eleven of us were billeted in a row of old almshouses in Bury St Edmunds. I was in a room with six other men, which made up a section. We had bunk beds with one lower berth and one upper berth which, of course, we tossed a coin for. I got the odd bed which was great except that it was at the far end of the room and if I came in late I had to be careful not to fall over anything or wake the others up. One day when it was my turn to clean the room out the platoon sergeant came in and on looking around said, 'So that's what you're up to. I've been looking all over the place for you. Didn't you see battalion orders for the day?'

This remark gave me quite a shock as all soldiers are supposed to study a notice board on which all duties for the day were posted, such as guard duties, cookhouse duties and many others. I naturally thought that I had missed seeing my name for some duty and had not reported to the orderly room for it. This was quite a serious offence in the army. He then told me that my name was on the notice board and putting his hand in his pocket, pulled a small packet out, handed it to me and told me to open it. When I opened it, there inside was one chevron, a lance corporal's stripe. He told me to sew them on as soon as possible. The official designation at that time was acting unpaid Lance Corporal which meant that I had the rank but not any extra pay. I was now officially a Section Commander, which meant that I was in charge of the men in my billet and certainly was not going to do any more cleaning duties. My father was very pleased about my promotion. Anyone would think I had been made an officer.

There were a number of other duties that I had become eligible for. I often found myself pushed into a sergeant's job. The rank had many benefits as we young NCOs were sent on many courses. One was run by the Royal Engineers on the use and handling of explosives. We had a lot of fun blowing up old tree stumps. The last exercise we did was mining a road for a tank trap. We prepared the mine and then the Royal Engineers towed an old tractor over the mine and up it went – very spectacular!

Gradually, all the men who had been called up at the same time as me were drafted into different companies. I was kept back to train men of each new intake as they arrived at the barracks. I also found my weekend duties getting far less as each week passed, so I followed the example of my fellow soldiers and managed to sneak home.

I travelled in a variety of ways. My best trip was in a chauffeur-driven limousine sitting next to a man who was far too interested in my army life. My worst trip was in a laundry van, sitting on baskets of washing in the back of the van and banging my head on the roof every time it went round a corner or over a bump. Wrapping my

23

head in an old towel helped to cushion the bumps. The coldest journey was in the sidecar of a motorcycle. The man was a plumber and used the sidecar to carry his tools. It was like a large box with no protection at all from the wind. But there were other problems – no one in the family knew when you were going to arrive. Some people got quite a shock to see their husbands standing on the doorstep.

The biggest problem was getting back to Bury St Edmunds. The fare from Liverpool Street Station was ten shillings. There was always a hurried consultation and whip-round to fund me back to Bury. All railway stations were closely watched by the Red Caps (Military Police) for deserters and people like me with no passes. Going through the barrier and onto the platform for the train was always quite a nerve-wracking time. An old soldier had told us of a trick he used. You hope to see an officer who is travelling on your train. As he approaches the barriers you keep as close to him as possible. If you are carrying a bag, better still, the Red Caps think you're his batman. I never tried it myself as one of the family always came onto the platform with me and that seemed to allay any suspicions that I had no pass.

Not too long after I had been made 5830401 A/Unpd L/Cpl P. R. Jackson, I became ill. I kept on vomiting, could not keep any food down, and was weak. I was shipped off to Colchester Military Hospital where I was diagnosed as having yellow jaundice, today known as hepatitis.

On my recovery, after spending six weeks in hospital, I was given a free pass to travel by train to Bury and after reporting to the appropriate authorities, was to be granted a week's sick leave and given a free return ticket to London. When I asked about my pay I was told that while I was in hospital my wife had applied for a hardship grant. The QSM told me that my pay was now to be reduced to three shillings and sixpence a week – a rate of sixpence per day!

I went home devastated and Margaret and I had a terrible argument. My wife told me that she had applied for more money because she was pregnant and not able to work. I asked her how long she had known she was expecting and she said a couple of months, but she wasn't sure. That sounded ambiguous but I didn't know that much about pregnant women so didn't question it. Mum was pleased but my Dad was furious. He said that she was going to bleed me of my army pay.

Chapter 5

Home Service

On 4 June 1940 I joined the other thousands of PBIs (poor bloody infantry) – the sacrificial troops to be sent into the melting pot each time someone had blundered. In actual fact, our battalion was fortunate because we spent some time in England on home service. I and a small detachment of men guarded British or German planes that had been shot down. The worst aspect of this was the behaviour of the civilian souvenir hunters. Frequently they were first on the scene and would strip the plane and even a dead body of anything that could be moved. Parachutes were very valuable as they were made of silk and I expect many women were married in wedding dresses made from some poor dead airman's parachute.

During the Battle of Britain I was with a detachment of troops guarding an RAF aerodrome near Southend. It was harrowing to see the condition of the airmen and their planes when they returned to base. Many were lifted from the cockpits and put onto stretchers. The planes were then patched up and sent off with another pilot. These boys did a great job saving Britain.

Next we were in the Norfolk Broads. My section was billeted in an old cottage next door to a pub. This sounds good, but the pub was 'out of bounds'. We were on full alert for an expected invasion and were expected to turn out at a moment's notice for any emergency. My section had to guard two bridges, one quite substantial, the other a small canal bridge that lifted in two sections to allow boats and barges to pass through. One evening an officer from the Royal Engineers showed up. Of course, we went through the usual routine of turning out the guard and seeing his credentials. It was his job to inspect the bridges every so often. The small one we were standing on was mined with enough gun ammunition to blow up the bridge and probably the pub as well. I asked him about the larger bridge and he said, 'Oh yes, that one packs a powerful punch too.' If the Germans invaded, these two bridges would be blown up.

Later we were on the east coast near Yarmouth, guarding against an invasion. Our billets this time were chalets belonging in peacetime to a holiday camp. We were still on full alert and my job was to ensure that the privates changed guard every two hours so that they were always alert. I was to be woken up at night at four-hourly intervals to patrol the two dugout positions on the top of the cliffs, to ensure they were manned at all times.

I was in my chalet one night and, much against the rules, had taken my boots off to rest my feet as they (my boots) had been on for about thirty-six hours. I was sitting in a chair with my back to the door when I awoke to feel something being poked into my back. It scared the living daylights out of me. Then a voice spoke and told me I was lucky he wasn't a German soldier. It was my Platoon Officer's baton being poked at me. He gave me a severe telling off for not being alert or properly dressed. I explained to him that only a very short time before his visit I had done my patrol of the area and had advised the sentries to call me out if anything suspicious was happening, but he made no comment and went on his way. I can assure you that patrolling a cliff path at 3.00am in pitch darkness, without even the light of the moon, is no joke. In the early hours of the morning, when one is very tired, the world takes on a strange quality. A small shrub or a tall plant seems almost like a person, or a sudden rustle of an animal can make one nervous.

On one particular night there was to my left a definite movement in a hedge and quick as a flash my safety-catch was off, and my finger on the trigger. On the command, 'Halt, who goes there?' a very low voice said, 'Duty Officer'.

My next order was, 'Advance and be recognized,' and out of the hedge stepped my officer. I could only dimly see his face but I recognized his voice. When he stepped forward we both realized that the muzzle of my rifle had been only inches away from his stomach. Neither he nor I made any comment at the time but he never tried to hide in a hedge again.

In July 1940 I was promoted once again, this time to Acting Corporal, which meant that there was no additional pay. It did, however, make life a little easier as I was able to delegate some duties to the new lance corporal. Not too long after my promotion I became a fully paid NCO and wore my second stripe with great pride when I went home on leave. My parents were proud of me and insisted that I have my photograph taken on my own. This did not impress my wife. She was even less impressed when I wouldn't tell her how much extra I was being paid.

After the Battle of Britain the threat of invasion became less and less likely and so we were stood down from full alert. I was still stationed near Norwich and on 20 July 1940 was informed that my wife had given birth to a son. Shortly after this event I was told that London was becoming unsafe owing to the start of the German air raids. It was suggested by the government that, if possible, civilians should be evacuated into the country.

As an NCO I was entitled to a sleeping-out pass as long as I was not scheduled for any duties at night. I heard from a friend that a certain lady was looking for a companion to share her house as her husband was away overseas. I went to see her and it was arranged for Margaret and Malcolm to be billeted at her house, which was a mere five minutes walk from my billet. Margaret was not enthusiastic about the idea, but after some bad air raids it became obvious London was dangerous. It was worse because we lived near a railway marshalling area, which were considered prime targets by the German bombers.

Owing to the delay in Margaret making up her mind, I had become quite friendly with Dorothy, who had a one-year-old daughter. I was often invited over for a meal and to play cards or draughts with her elderly grandfather. The old man usually went to bed at about 9.30pm and this left us on our own to chat and have tea or cocoa. On odd occasions I would call into the pub and buy a bottle of cider to share with her and Grandad.

One evening Dorothy said she was going to do some baby washing and asked me how we soldiers managed with washing our clothes. I told her that ours were bundled up once a week and went to a laundry. I then mentioned that when our underwear came back it felt as though it had been starched and took a whole day to become comfortable. She was very sympathetic and suggested that for a small sum she would do my washing for me. It so happened that my laundry was due to be sent that next morning. She told me to go and fetch it and let her wash it for me as a free trial. This I did, and then she asked me about the clothes I was wearing. Of course, I laughed and made some sort of joke about going back to my billet with no underwear on. She then said that there would be no need to go back to my billet. Her bed was very comfortable and she thought we both needed the companionship. My underwear did get washed and that is, perhaps, all I need to say.

Shortly after this Margaret went to live with her and life became complicated. Dorothy gave up her double bed to Margaret and me. Margaret thought that because I had a sleeping-out pass, the army was a nine-to-five job. It soon became obvious that she expected me to be home every night and couldn't understand why sometimes I only got home one night in three. Dorothy started picking on Margaret for many little things and, eventually, the truth came out. She resented my being in England while her husband was overseas. But by this time I was on my way to Scotland so knew little about it.

Chapter 6

Bonny Scotland

We left to go north at midday in the middle of winter. The next morning someone asked where I thought we were. I probably said something like, 'God only knows'. It was then that we heard some men working on the line close by. One of our number put his head out of the window and called out, 'Hey, mate, where are we?'

We heard someone clear his throat and then the distinct sound of a spit on the ground and something he said sounded like, 'Hoik'.

'Look mate, I know you're bloody 'hoiking', but where the hell are we?'

This time it was a different Scottish voice. 'Y'ere in Scotland. The place is called Hoik, HAWICK if you want it spelt out – ye daft Sassenach.'

When we arrived at the station we were marched out and were amazed at the amount of snow. We marched for approximately five miles and reached an army camp with a number of wooden huts that were to be our homes. At first sight it looked a cold cheerless place, snow everywhere and the huts were quite drab looking, unpainted, weather-boarded.

We later learnt that they had been used in the 1914–1918 war as an army camp and had, supposedly, been renovated for our battalion. The place was called Stobbs Camp.

Each platoon was allocated a hut, and we found that each one had a potbelly stove in the centre. There was a race to see who could grab a bed nearest the stove. We were issued with a coal bucket and shovel and taken to a large heap of wood and coal. We were to keep our own huts supplied with fuel. It was not too long before we made ourselves at home and comfortable. We had become a tough lot and had got quite accustomed to sleeping anywhere and living rough.

Our training consisted of open country warfare and lots of route marches, all done in snow. Soon after we arrived we were ordered to parade in winter wear, which meant long woollen underpants were to be worn under our battledress and greatcoats.

Off we went on our march and we were told it was an exercise that could last two days, which is why we had to be warmly dressed. We had not gone too far when I started to sweat and then I started to itch; very soon the itching became an extreme irritation. There was no way of scratching or rubbing my legs as the greatcoat covered most of my body. Fortunately, on a route march the rule is a ten-minute break in every hour. Also, the regulation pace is approximately four miles per hour. Our first break gave me a chance to cool off. Very shortly after the break we were dispersed to various defensive positions and informed that we were being attacked by an enemy.

I set my men out in their various places and then retired to the nearest clump of bushes in sight where I took off my trousers and underpants. This is difficult in army uniform. My army boots were a size eleven and over the boots were a pair of gaiters. When I finally got the pants off and saw my body it was as if I had been badly sunburnt – I was allergic to woollen underwear.

Our day started at reveille 6.00am and unless we had evening duties we were free after the evening meal which was at about 5.30pm. The camp held no attraction for us and most men walked the five miles to Hawick with ease. The local people were good company and we soon made friends with some who invited us to their homes. The dances at the Town Hall were very popular, as was the picture theatre; pubs did a good trade, so too the local canteen that had been set up by the ladies of the town.

I had only been in Hawick a short time when I met a girl, or should I say bumped into a girl, who was walking past. It was a heavy bump and I was very apologetic and started to talk. Before I knew it, I was seeing her home. Our friendship developed and we went to dances and pictures together. One night I could not deceive her any longer and told her I was married. She then confessed that she had never introduced me to her family because she had a boyfriend overseas. Usually I would see her home and we would have a kiss and cuddle on the doorstep and that was as far as it went; it was a kind of unspoken agreement.

Mary's father was the local policeman. One night I took her home and there he was, standing at the gate. He told Mary to go into the house because he wanted a few words with me. He began by saying (in a Scots brogue), 'So you're the married man my daughter has been going around with. I don't want you around my house any more. She's already betrothed to someone else and if he finds out about you, you'll be in a lot of trouble. So you begone and if I see you with her again I'll be after you with a garden rake.' I can assure you that there was no argument from me.

Mary and I met one final time to say goodbye. I asked how her father had found out about us going together. It appeared that a neighbour's son had been home on leave and had seen us at the cinema together. He had told his mother and, in turn, she had passed it to Mary's mother.

Later I met Margaret. She was prepared to go to the pictures with me, but said her mother would be very worried if she stayed out without letting her know where she was. 'If it's alright, I'll meet you outside the cinema at seven o'clock.' If she hadn't arrived by then I was not to wait but go in on my own.

At five minutes to seven, she arrived and we spent our first evening together. After the film she allowed me to see her home. She was a wee pixie of a thing, as pretty as a picture and always laughing. I fell in love with her. We spent more and more time together, mostly just walking the hills and talking. Often she would shout me to the cinema or buy me a meal. I really loved her but knew it was all wrong as I was a married man.

It was probably on a Sunday that she announced that her mother wanted to meet me. This came as a shock. I knew her mother was a widow. I also knew that she was a nurse at the Galasheils Hospital. I went to tea that evening. Margaret's mother was a very pleasant lady and treated me very kindly but I still could not pluck up the courage to confess that I was married.

As to my marital situation, as all ex-servicemen know, one has to go on Pay Parade. Your name is called: 5830401 Cpl Jackson P.R., step forward, salute the officer, hand over your pay book, they check it, hand you your pay, one step back, salute the officer, and dismiss yourself. This particular day I collected my pay and, horror of horrors, it was exactly half of my usual amount. My wife had done it again; she got more, I got less.

One morning I read Battalion Orders and my name was there to report to the Orderly Room at 0900 hours. I went, wondering what the hell I had done now. When I arrived I was told that I had been made Corporal in charge of messing arrangements. I was excused all duties – no more route marches, no more parades, no more fatigues. It was a very responsible job, they said.

It seemed that a lot of complaints had been made by the civilian population about the amount of wasted food that had been seen coming from some army establishments. My job was to look into the matter and report to a duty officer who would be appointed each day. I had no jurisdiction over the cookhouse staff, nor was I able to give any direct orders to anyone senior to me such as the quartermaster who ordered the supplies or the cookhouse sergeant. I could, however, report any wastage that was occurring.

It soon became clear that breakfast was not a problem, as all the men were in camp and had to eat in the mess halls. The same also applied to lunch or, as we called it, dinner, except on Saturdays and Sundays. Most wastage occurred at weekends and in the evening meals. Every man wanted to get into town and have a meal if he could afford it. This meant that half the food that was prepared finished up in the pigswill.

The mess halls had tables that seated eight men per table. The midday meal was served up individually to each man. It was usually a stew, potatoes, vegetables and gravy, and a sweet of some kind. The evening meal was served differently. A loaf of bread or perhaps two loaves were placed on each table, a pound packet of butter, possibly a tin of herrings in tomato sauce or a large piece of cheese, sometimes a tin of corned beef and, on odd occasions, even some ham had been known to appear. This last item probably came from the officers' mess and had gone off a bit so they gave it to us instead of the pigs. There was also a dish of jam. Instead of eight men sitting at each table the men present had been splitting up into small groups of, perhaps, five at one table, three at another table and so on. So, instead of one tin of something between eight men most of it was wasted, as was the bread.

My first two tasks had immediate results. The first was to make sure that eight men were seated at each table. The second was to try and establish the number of men in camp on Saturday and Sunday for meals. It soon became apparent that catering for two-thirds of the men would be more than adequate. My next assignment was to check the dry goods store and bread and butter cool rooms.

Bread was ordered on a daily basis and was supposed to be used strictly in rotation. My first visit to the bread store was quite horrifying. The bread was kept on open shelves with no protection. I noticed a pile of crumbs on the floor of the storeroom and, on closer inspection, I found that they were coming from a row of loaves directly above. I lifted two or three loaves on the shelf to inspect them and, apart from being as hard as bricks, they had no inside to them. I took further loaves off the shelf and eventually found that a rat, or rats, had steadily eaten their way through about six loaves of bread. I also found that the bread had not been used in rotation. No wonder there had been complaints about stale or mouldy bread.

I had things running quite smoothly at the camp and thought I would be sent back to my unit but, somehow, there was always something else. Although only a corporal, I must have relieved some people senior to me of some quite onerous duties and so they kept me on.

Quite often, there would be perhaps half-a-pound of butter left on my table, also a nice piece of cheese, or even an unopened tin of sardines or herrings. I was still seeing Margaret as she would taxi out to me and we would walk in the hills. One evening I slipped a tin of herrings into my pocket. I went into town that night and asked Margaret if she thought her mother would like the tin. From then on I kept some butter and other odds and ends back after meals and put them in my gas mask bag. I only took food that had not been mutilated and was perfectly clean.

One evening Margaret came out in a taxi and said that I had been invited to visit some friends of hers. I wasn't very keen on this as I was very conscious of being married and didn't want to stir up any trouble. I had put one or two items in my bag for Margaret and so we visited friends and had a great evening. I often gave Margaret different items but she started to give me money in exchange. It appeared that gradually people were telling one another about their gifts and it was developing into a sort of black market. Goodness knows I could well use the odd few shillings I was given but my common sense told me this would get me into trouble, so I stopped the whole thing.

At this time I thought it was prudent to tell Margaret that I was a married man. We had been to the cinema that night and I said that there was something that she should know about me. I was very nervous and upset at the thought of confessing. Before I had time to blurt it all out, she told me that she had known for ages that I was married. Mary had met her and told her about me. Margaret then explained that we had meant so much to each other that she couldn't bear to tell me. She knew that sooner or later we would have to part as I would probably be sent overseas. She told me that she had guessed that I was married even before Mary had told her. I asked her, 'What made you think that was the case?'

'You were always short of money but tried not to let me see.' She had bought me a small gold signet ring and asked me to wear it for good luck and to think of her sometimes. I had to say goodbye to Margaret two days later. It was 1941.

We marched to the railway station and were on our way to somewhere in England or Wales, or perhaps even France or Norway. When we finished our journey we were in Herefordshire, near the town.

Before I left Hawick my wife had posted a letter, which had been forwarded on to Hereford. The letter informed me that owing to the bombing in London she had again been evacuated to the country. She had written to her old guardian at Ross-on-Wye and had been told she was very welcome to stay with her as long as she wished. It was only a short bus ride between the camp at which I was stationed and Ross-on-Wye, so when Margaret (my wife) heard this she was delighted. I don't think that I was particularly overjoyed as I was missing Scotland. I did my husbandly duties and visited her as frequently as I could and then the subject of a sleeping-out pass came up. Fortunately, my duties were such that once a week was about the best I could manage and so on those occasions Auntie slept on the couch and my wife and I shared a double bed. My son had a cot in the same room as us. By the time he had been looked after and finally settled down, I was so fed up that I wished I was back in camp.

My wife took it for granted that she had a full-time husband. Orders were made, 'Next time you come, would you bring so-and-so,' or, 'I could do with this, or that'. I rarely complied with these instructions as whatever money I spent was never repaid. Then came the orders such as, 'Oh Peter, while you're here, I'll get you to go down to the shop and take the baby for a walk.' I found that to be given instructions by a woman who seemed to be on holiday with very little to do was a blow to my ego. A soldier in uniform pushing a baby in a pram around a small country village was a figure of fun in those days. Gradually my visits to my wife became less and less frequent as I began to find excuses not to go.

After a time, discipline became stricter and guard duties more vigilant. The officers seemed to have a new sense of purpose and our training schedules were increased. One morning we looked at Battalion Orders and there were instructions that we were to parade and be ready for inspection by the Battalion Commander. We had been through all this caper before. Usually we stood to attention for a couple of hours and never saw anyone of importance. This particular day we were called to attention, then came the order, 'Slope arms', next, 'Present arms'. We all stood rock steady like statues as we saw His Majesty King George VI and the Colonel of the Regiment. Every now and again the king would stop and have a word with one of the men until finally the parade was over. My only recollection is that my eyes were firmly fixed in the eyes front position and I looked right over the king's head.

We were given seven days embarkation leave, some of which I spent in London with Mum and Dad and the rest at Ross-on-Wye. I said my goodbyes and I was once more on a troop train, but this time it was only the prelude to the longer journey.

Chapter 7

Off Overseas

We were taken by train to Liverpool, arriving at night. My recollections of that day are like a dream. In no time we felt the throbbing of the engines and were on our way across the Atlantic Ocean. The ship was the *Andes*. It was a shallow draught vessel as it had been built for the River Plate traffic. We were warned to expect a rough trip; the weather in November in the North Atlantic is notoriously bad. The whole of the ship's company was on full alert as German submarines were active and so all troops were warned to watch out for anything suspicious.

After the first night I started to enjoy myself on board the ship. There were duty-free cigarettes, sweets and chocolate to purchase. There were some things that we had not seen in the shops for years. As the army had short paid me for about a year-and-a-half, I was able to board the ship with about £6 tucked away in my pockets.

After the first full day at sea we struck gale force winds and the ship rolled badly. Fortunately, I was a good sailor, but many others were very seasick, even senior officers and NCOs. The captain of the ship blamed much of the seasickness on the cheap chocolate and cigarettes and threatened to close the ship's canteen.

In the early hours of the fifth morning we docked in Halifax, Nova Scotia. We only knew our whereabouts by asking a local dock worker. Our expectations of visiting Canada were dashed when we found ourselves being shepherded down the *Andes'* gangplank, across the quayside and up another gangplank onto a much larger ship. I had only spent fifteen minutes on Canadian soil. I remember seeing hundreds of bags of shelled peanuts on the wharf. A good many of the bags were split open and the peanuts were strewn all over the place. As we shuffled our way across the wharf to go aboard the other ship, we stuffed handfuls of nuts into our pockets.

After we tasted them, we rapidly emptied our pockets – the nuts were rancid and full of mildew.

When I finally boarded the other ship I was most surprised to hear instructions being issued by an officer in a smart naval uniform. He was unmistakably American. We were put into groups of six or eight men and one man was given a numbered ticket. We then followed a sailor down totally bewildering passageways and stairways.

The sailor showed us into a cabin and demonstrated how the six bunk beds were to be folded up during the daytime and let down at night. The bunks were in tiers of three, one above the other on opposite walls of the cabin. The lower one was about 30cm from the floor, the second and third arranged so that the person on the lower bunk could sit up without striking his head. Each cabin had an electric fan and a wash basin, which was not be used as water was severely restricted. Showers and ablution facilities were communal, as were the heads (toilets). He also warned us not to open the porthole, which was impossible anyway, as it was welded shut, but at least, we could see daylight through it. We were to stay in our cabin until we heard from our own officers.

Later we were told it was 'chow time' (grub up) and we found our way to the dining hall. We queued up not knowing what to expect. The food on the *Andes* had been the usual Army mush so we quite expected the same on this ship. We picked up a metal tray with several divisions in it and we passed a line of cooks serving food. Something different was plonked in each division on the tray and we then went to a waist-high bench with our tray and utensils and ate standing up. Surprisingly, it was a marvellous meal. Afterwards there was tea or coffee on tap; we hadn't tasted coffee like that for years.

Near evening, we heard a new sound, a steady hum and the ship began to vibrate slightly. Gradually the noise and vibration increased and we knew we were moving. I can still remember the feeling of foreboding and the despondency that came over me as we left the dockside. We were going into the unknown

Once the ship was underway we decided to explore the area around our cabin. We soon found some of our comrades in the other cabins nearby and things began to brighten up. Finally, we all drifted back to our cabins and settled down for the night. The next morning we were rudely awakened, not by our usual reveille, but by a trumpet blaring out the Bugle Call Rag through the public address system that was installed throughout the ship. An American sailor came along past the cabins calling out such things as, 'Get off your bunks you bloody Limeys,' or, 'Wakey, wakey, sons of bitches.' I think whoever he was he must have gone through the officers' quarters because we were never treated to that experience again.

After our ablutions it was chow time. Then we were told which Company would parade on deck at 0930 hours for inspection. My cabin was included in the first detail so we proceeded to the designated deck. Our usual morning inspection involved checking we were shaved and clean, that our uniform was complete, and no-one was sick or had fallen overboard in the night. We were then told to stand fast as the captain of the ship wished to speak to us.

'Hear ye, hear ye, the smoking lamp is lit on the port side. I repeat, the smoking lamp is lit on the port side. Attention all British troops, this means that you may smoke on the left-hand side of the ship facing forward, which, by the way, is the bow of the ship. You may only smoke when the order comes through on the PA system and no-one, I repeat, no-one is allowed to smoke below decks. Certain areas of the ship are designated for smoking and, as you have just heard, are preceded by the words, "The smoking lamp is lit in whichever area I say".'

We then had a lecture on the ship's geography and one of the crew took parties of twelve men at a time on a tour. We were all very impressed when we were shown deck-mounted machineguns and light AKA (anti-aircraft guns) with multiple barrels, which could fire about twelve or more shots at one time. We would be manning these guns in company with the Americans day and night. Finally we were shown two large 6in guns mounted on the forward deck of the ship and were informed by our guide that, 'If ever they have to fire those bloody guns they'll probably tear themselves out of the deck because this old tub wasn't built for that sort of a job.' We hoped that those guns would never be fired because it would mean we were in big trouble.

The wartime name of the ship was the *Wakefield*. In peacetime it had been a cruise ship and was irreverently known as a floating brothel, otherwise called the *Manhattan*. We had noticed a large number of erotic paintings adorning the walls and ceiling in the dining hall. This caused our lads a lot of amusement and many ribald remarks were made.

For the first few days of the voyage there were always some new instructions to obey such as: 0900 hours all D Company personnel will parade on Deck 'A' for physical training, or weapons training. We had earlier on been designated our assembly points and lifeboat stations. We also were obliged to carry our life jackets with us at all times. We had been instructed in how to wear them. The particular type the British troops were issued with resembled two pillows fitted in front on the chest and the other at the back of the head just below the neck. Once the life jacket was tied on I could not bend my head forward without feeling strangled by it. Our instructor told us that if we had to abandon ship, we should not jump feet first because the life jacket would come under your chin and probably break your neck. Someone asked what would happen if we jumped overboard head first. I don't think he answered that question.

As this was a troopship and we were in dangerous waters at the time, emergency drills were a frequent occurrence. Although we thought, 'Oh no, not another bloody boat drill,' there was always the nasty feeling that one day we would feel the thump of a torpedo.

American and British troops were posted at strategic positions around the ship. When on night watch we had to parade in one of the lounges fully kitted out with life jackets. The American officer then called the roll both for us and the American sailors. Most of the Brits were read out as: Jackson, Brown, Jones, Williams, Johnson, and so on. The Americans had such names as Guggenheimer, Schmidt, Schenk, and quite a few others I won't even attempt to spell. There was the odd Jones or Jackson and, strangely, they seemed to be black men.

On night watch I was posted forward of the ship not too far away from the bow. I was on a small platform jutted out from the side of the ship with a guardrail round it. There was also a machine gun mounted on the platform. I accompanied an American sailor who was in charge of the gun. There was no protection from the elements and although it didn't rain, it was freezing cold in the biting wind. We stood two-hour watches with two hours off. It was great to be able to go inside and my comrade took me to the galley where there was a great vat of hot coffee. This was real American coffee – one cup of it and you were suddenly wide awake. We always reckoned the Yanks put some dope in it.

We settled down quite well to cruising the ocean. We were able to buy cigarettes and other items from our canteen at duty-free prices.

The Americans had their own canteen and they were able to buy all sorts of cigarettes that we had never heard of. Cigars were smoked by even the lowliest members of the crew and it was every Brit's ambition to become the friend of a Yank. As long as we had some money, the Americans could buy us cigarettes, cigars and, best of all, candy bars. My cabin mates were lucky as we chummed up with a sailor who had spent some time in London and married an English girl, and so we had a lot in common.

We were disappointed when we were once again served by our own army cooks. It was back to the same old greasy stews, watery soups and soggy boiled spuds. Desserts were so-called rice puddings. The British Government had agreed to feed us and the Americans were not responsible for our welfare as we had our own chain of command.

The hundreds of men on the ship had no idea where we were sailing. Whether our officers knew our destination, I don't know. We asked our sailor friend if he knew and he said, 'Your guess is as good as mine'. One thing we had noticed was that each day the weather was getting warmer and the sea calmer. We felt that other than the daily parades or duties we really were on a cruise.

My mates and I were lucky that our six-berth cabin had a fan. Further down below decks and below the waterline men were living and sleeping in dormitory-like accommodation, fifty or sixty men to a cabin. Gradually, our cabin began to get uncomfortably warm and when we switched on the fan it would not oscillate. It just blew out a blast of cold air so we had to put up with the heat. Somehow a rumour started that we were sailing through the Mediterranean Sea. Then we believed that we were going to Italy.

One day a sailor came to our cabin and said, 'OK, you's guys, you've seen your last daylight,' and proceeded to paint our porthole glass black. It was obvious that the ship was being blacked out. Again, I got that funny feeling in the pit of my stomach and the thought that now things were going to happen.

Next day on deck someone said he thought he could see land ahead. Very soon it was obvious and then the captain's voice came over the PA system ordering all troops below decks. Shortly after that the ship gradually stopped. We knew she had dropped anchor and all sorts of things were happening up above us. Gradually things quietened down and we were allowed on deck. We could see what we later learned were liberty boats taking sailors back and forth to shore. At last we were given some information. We had arrived in Trinidad in the West Indies and would remain anchored about one or two miles off the coast for supplies, fuel and water. British soldiers would be asked to perform certain duties. American sailors and personnel would be granted shore leave, but no British. We did see a lot of British officers mingling with the Yanks in the liberty boats though. Trapped aboard the ship, seeing the lights at night, hearing the noise of music and seeing the sailors coming and going; we were all fed up.

On odd occasions we saw some sailors being brought aboard the ship either bandaged up or, in some cases, on stretchers. When we enquired what had happened to them we were told that they had ignored advice on certain places they should not visit and had been beaten up and robbed.

We stayed in Trinidad for probably three days and then, once again, set off into the unknown. Once we left Trinidad the weather became hotter and the cabin was very uncomfortable. Permission was given that a certain number of men could sleep on deck at night. There were no particular instructions regarding who or where. It was a case of taking our blankets on deck in the evening and choosing a spot to sleep. When I said we slept on deck, I meant just that. We lay on one blanket and covered ourselves with the other one. We had no mattresses on the bunks in the cabin, just a canvas base, so the deck was not much harder to sleep on than our bunks.

Chapter 8

Cape Town

Gradually we approached land and it soon became apparent that this time we were going to dock. This caused great excitement. Then an order came over the PA system that personnel were under no circumstances to crowd the starboard side, thereby upsetting the balance of the ship.

Once the ship had docked and was secured, we were ordered on deck and our officers told us that we were in Cape Town for approximately four days and would be allowed a certain amount of shore leave. At that news a big cheer went up. There would be company pay parades, the first since leaving England. At that news an even bigger cheer went up. Before we left our sergeant said, 'Don't forget boys, you're here to show the flag for England.' As had happened to the Americans in Trinidad, we had been warned to be careful where we went and where we drank and, of course, to be more than careful if we indulged in sexual exploits.

On my first day ashore I was on my own. My mates were either on duty or were bound for the nearest pub. Pubs were not my scene and I preferred walking around the city sightseeing. Also, I had not been paid out much money as my wife had grabbed most of my wage. Around midday I found a rather nice café bar facing onto the sea front and, as it wasn't all that expensive, decided to have a drink. There were several civilians sitting around. I had been served with my drink but was still not sure about lunch, debating whether I could afford it or not.

A young man who was about my own age had been sitting nearby. Picking up his drink he came over to my table and said, 'Excuse me, but are you off the ship that has just come in?' He introduced himself as John. I told him that I was but I was unable to give him any information about the journey we were on. He told me that he wasn't looking for that sort of conversation and asked if we

42

could chat about England for a while. I told him that I was from London and at this he got quite excited and said, 'Please don't go away as my wife, Anne, is from London and would love to hear some of its news.'

The woman had lived with her parents at Finchley before the war. I knew the area quite well and was able to assure her that when I left England very little damage had been done to that area. John had been born in South Africa and had visited England and had some of his education there. He had met Anne and they had fallen in love. John had returned to South Africa while Anne had stayed with her parents in London. John had been hoping to return to London at a later date so that they could marry but as the threat of war loomed larger and larger, and in the end seemed inevitable, Anne's parents were almost insistent that she would be better off going to South Africa and getting married there. She had left England only a few days before war was declared.

I told them about myself, but I was beginning to feel uncomfortable in their company as I had very little money to return their hospitality. I was more or less prepared to leave them when John must have read my thoughts. He offered to buy my lunch if I would care to stay and talk to some other people that they knew. Eventually, Anne returned with a couple who were a little older than John and Anne. We were introduced to each other and, once again, there were lots of questions about England, and London in particular. I learnt that the older couple were relations of John who lived in Johannesburg but were spending a holiday in Cape Town. Later in the afternoon I explained to John that I had to be back on board the ship by 6.00pm as I was on picket duty that evening.

It was at this point that the older man came up with a rather astounding suggestion. He said that in Johannesburg they were very short of white skilled workers. I seemed a bright sort of chap and would be ideal for him to employ as an overseer in his business. His suggestion was that if I decided it was worthwhile I should, as he put it, 'jump ship,' and he would assure me 'a good job in Johannesburg, no questions asked'. It was arranged that I could meet with John and Anne the next day and let them know if I was interested in this suggestion.

I got back to the ship and, naturally, thought about it for most of the evening. Had I been single I think I might have been tempted to consider his offer but, being married, it was impossible. My wife would have had her allowance stopped as I would have been posted as a deserter. In all probability I would never have been able to return to England. The more I thought about, the more I thought it a stupid, impossible idea. It also occurred to me that the person who had suggested deserting had taken rather a risk. I couldn't help wondering what would happen if I told one of our officers what had taken place.

The next day my cabin mates were all off duty and so we went out sightseeing and kept well clear of the hotel where I was to meet John and Anne. On the night before our departure our group decided to make a night of it. One of the American sailors had told us of this fabulous place called Del Monico, so we decided to go there. I had been very economical with my money and so could afford a night out.

My memory of Del Monico is misty. I remember going into this rather grandiose place full of Americans and British officers and finding a table. One of our party went to the bar and came back with some drinks, remarking that all that stuff up there on the top shelf was only sixpence a glass. Somehow it was decided that we would start at the beginning and work our way along the shelf. To this day I have no idea of how many drinks I had. I have only a memory of some men coming into a lavatory, picking me up and carrying me outside, then climbing into some sort of horse carriage and careering along a road with a bell clanging and a lot of laughing.

I vaguely remember being led down some passages and presumably put onto my bunk; anyway, that's where I was when I awoke in the morning. I lay on my bunk for a while and felt no ill effects from the previous night and so decided to get up. I swung my legs over the side of the bunk and stood up. The cabin whirled round and round and I fell flat on my face on the floor. Fortunately, no major damage was done, only a nosebleed. It was two or three days before I felt well again.

Chapter 9

India – 29 October 1941

When we arrived in Bombay we were told to disembark as this was the end of our journey. We left the ship and joined our units as sections, platoons and companies. Once we had sorted ourselves out, we were marched to some waiting railway carriages and so moved from troop ship to troop train in a very short space of time.

I had seen Halifax, Nova Scotia, in the blink of an eye and now the same thing was happening in Bombay. The things I most remember were the throngs of people, the noise of hundreds of voices all jabbering at the same time, the indefinable smell and the heat.

We waited on the train, seated on hard wooden benches. The train chugged along and we passed station after station thronged with Indians. Eventually we reached the end of the journey.

Once we had formed up in our units and had roll calls, we marched to an army camp called Ahmadnagar, about 120 miles from Bombay. It was a fairly basic sort of a camp. We had huts to sleep in, the usual trough-type ablutions, benches and smelly latrines, plus, of course, the inevitable parade ground. This consisted of a large quadrangle of dusty soil set in the centre of the huts and administration buildings.

We were allocated our huts and then came the usual discussion about who was going to sleep where. This was solved by the first one in the hut chucking his gear on the bed he fancied. I got the bed nearest the door which proved to be a mixed blessing. I got a lot of cool air but a lot of dust as well.

A number of our senior NCOs were old soldiers who had already been stationed in India. They were able to advise us on a few basic rules: 'Tip your boots upside down before you put them on at any time. There may be scorpions or other nasty things hiding in them. Never leave anything of value where the Indians can see it. They'll grab it as soon as look at it.'

The cookhouse was a good way from our hut and to get to it we had to cross the parade ground – or so we thought. We left our hut and started out for our midday meal. Halfway across the parade ground we heard the roar of the Sergeant Major's voice shouting at us. He was telling us in no uncertain terms that on no account were we to cross the 'red blooded' parade ground unless we were on duty, or at drill. This made it a long trip to the food station. We took our mess tins and the food was dished up and then carried back to be eaten in our huts. By this time it was nearly cold.

One other hazard was the kite-hawks that flew continuously overhead. If you neglected to cover your meal, these birds could swoop down and in the blink of an eye half your meal was snatched from your plate.

As is usual in the army, we settled in to the routines of drill, route marches, parades and guard duty, although we had no idea what we were guarding. It is quite amazing how the men who command troops can find so many useless ways of using up time and energy in an effort to teach us discipline and physical fitness.

As I have said previously, a few of our NCO's were old soldiers, not in the sense of age, but regular soldiers who had served in the Indian peacetime army. It didn't take them long to organize the Indian camp followers, who had all kinds of odd duties.

We had a Chai Wallah who carried a large pot of tea that was kept continually hot by a small charcoal brazier built into the base of the pot. In the hot climate, he was in constant demand as we were always ready for a cup of chai. It cost about two annas per cup which in today's British currency would be about one pence.

We were paid in Indian rupees and when we spent money in the camp canteen, we always finished up with a lot of small change, particularly one and two anna coins. We found these were very acceptable to some of the older 'boys' who frequented the camp. They were always willing to clean our boots or polish our buttons or run small errands for a small sum of money. We also attempted to learn a few words of the Indian language, which seemed to be understood by the Indians and got things done in a hurry. The small amount of money we gave to the locals was much appreciated and some of them became quite friendly, at least as friendly as we could allow them to be under the circumstances.

As is always the case, the senior members of the battalion were far better off than us junior NCOs and privates. The officers had their own mess, as did the sergeants. Indian waiters were employed on a full-time basis in these places. In peacetime, a great number of Indians were employed both by the British Army and the civilian authorities. Indians who were employed, even at a low level, were respected men in their own community and competition was fierce to get a job with the British.

We saw a lot of poverty when we did our route marches of about ten miles out into the country. It was nothing we could do anything about. The scale of the problem was just so vast.

Unfortunately, the main township was out of bounds to ORs (other ranks). However, we were allowed to visit a bazaar about fifteen minutes walk away from the barracks and this gave us the opportunity to see and buy a lot of handcrafts and fine silks. I managed to buy my wife a nice silk dressing gown, with an Indian dragon woven in gold thread on the back, which I hoped I would be able to give her at some time.

One afternoon our company was assembled and we were treated to an Indian magic show. These men really mystified us. One of our own men was selected from the audience and hypnotized into being absolutely rigid, he was then placed horizontally between two chairs. A large stone was then placed on his chest and a man smashed it to pieces with a big hammer. He was then stood up again and returned to normal. When questioned, he swore that he could remember nothing at all. The medical officer examined him, expecting to find at least bruising to his chest, but no signs of any damage were found.

Three Indian fakirs took part in the show, each one doing something different. One pushed large needles into his cheeks and tongue and other parts of his body. He walked amongst us to let us see him. He then went back on to the stage and on removing them invited an officer to inspect him to see any signs of where they had penetrated. The officer said he could see no blood or other signs of wounds.

Another of the fakirs passed round a bowl of uncooked rice for us to see and feel. He then placed a tripod arrangement on the head of one of our men, put the bowl of rice on the tripod and added cold water to it. After a few minutes steam began rising from the bowl. Later he came down from the stage and took the bowl of rice off the man's head, wrapping a towel round the base. It was then passed around several rows of men for them to test whether it was cooked.

The verdict was: yes, it was cooked rice. Before removing the tripod from the man's head, the fakir inserted an ordinary light bulb into it. This immediately lit up. I had it on good authority that from then on the man became known as 'Live Wire' to his mates.

We experienced the richness and colour of various Indian festivals. There were obviously some extremely rich men judging by the opulent displays of jewellery and wealth we saw. I could not help thinking that if even a small amount of their wealth was taken from them to help the poverty-stricken people that we saw near our camp, it would have made a world of difference to those poor beggars. In reality those people were little different from the poor people who had previously lived in the English slums.

We, at the bottom of the heap in the army, had no idea at all what we were doing in India. It was surmised that as the Japanese had invaded China we were bound for that theatre of war. We were never sure what was going on. In the past when we had trained in Scotland in mid-winter, we had heard through the grapevine that we could be bound for Norway, but here we were in India.

I remember my birthday in India because about this time (between Christmas 1941 and 4 January 1942) rumours started to circulate that we would soon be on the move again. Not long after this we marched down the dusty road to the railway station, boarded a train to Bombay, then marched down to the docks to our same American ships. We were ordered to board the ships and take up positions in our previous berths and I had a real reunion with my old cabin mates.

We learnt that the Japanese had bombed Pearl Harbour and so America was now at war with the Japanese. Security and discipline on the ship was much stricter and we were far more alert when we were scheduled to be on watch.

Eventually we learnt that we were going to Singapore as reinforcement troops to combat the Japanese invasion. Shortly after this we were put on red alert, for we were approaching the Japanese war zone. Our convoy was going to pass through the Straits of Malacca which divide Malaya and Sumatra. There we had the first taste of live action and shots from our guns were fired in anger.

Early in the morning the first 'Action Stations' call came as our ship was attacked by a number of Japanese planes. We had heard our anti-aircraft guns being fired in practice, but this was a completely new experience. The whole ship seemed to shudder and, at the same time, the Jap bombs were exploding in the water all around us. The attack did not last long and we sustained no damage either to our ship or to personnel. Later in the day there was another attack with the same result. I later heard that one of the ships in the convoy was sunk, apparently the one containing the transport and supplies.

After safely negotiating the Straits of Malacca we finally docked at Singapore. It was obvious that the Japanese were active as we could clearly hear the thump-thump of exploding bombs. There was so much going on at the docks that it was difficult to take it all in, but my first impression was of the number of people waiting to get on the ships that we were disembarking from. The island was being evacuated.

Chapter 10

Singapore –
The Island Fortress?

What seemed like turmoil to us soldiers was really organized chaos. Riding up and down the wharf were men on box tricycles selling such things as ice cream, pineapple juice, soft drinks and even food.

At some time during the day we were taken to a village, which was to be our headquarters. One of our first tasks was to uncoil rolls and rolls of barbed wire along the whole length of a beautiful beach. We were told that this had not been done before as it would have upset the civilian people who used the beach. On other beaches, troops were doing the same, whilst others were building tank traps and fortifications at different places around the island.

To us newcomers it appeared that not a great deal had been done to secure the island except from a seaborne invasion. Of course, we had heard about the great guns and defences on the seaward side, but the Japs were not coming that way. They were doing the impossible: coming down through the Malayan jungle.

We were confined to this small village, composed of thatched huts in the middle of nowhere, going out on working parties each day. At times we met up with some other soldiers who had been in Singapore for some time. They told us of the pleasures of the city and of the wonderful night life of the New World, the Great World and the Raffles Hotel, which were full of lovely Singaporean girls.

One of our duties was to patrol a road nearby to check on the comings and goings of the civilians and to see if they had seen any Japanese. They were Singaporeans, Malayans, Chinese, Indians and others we didn't recognize, so how on earth were we to know who were Japanese?

It was while I was on one of these patrols that we heard the distant sound of gunfire. The Japs were getting nearer and before the day was out I saw the first wounded men being brought along the road in ambulances. It was quite a frightening thing to see a convoy of field ambulances coming towards you and as they passed you, to catch sight of men with bloody bandages on all parts of their bodies. Even worse to see the feet of men on stretchers loosely moving from side to side as the ambulance drove along. As I looked I could only wonder whether they were alive or dead.

The Japs had reached Johor Bahru and only a strip of water separated them from Singapore Island. There was also the famous causeway linking the island to Malaya, which was supposed to be destroyed in case of invasion. The sounds of the battle were coming closer and it was evident that the Japanese had crossed to Singapore. Our company was now on the move into the battle zone.

One of the duties of an NCO is to take a party of men on patrol duties. I was delegated to take my section on a reconnaissance patrol to see if there were any enemy in the area. I was in the lead. Another man followed me who leap-frogged ahead when I needed a break. Four other men would give covering fire if we met an enemy patrol and there was one man who stayed in the rear. His job was to retreat as quickly as possible to take back any information as to where we had met the enemy. This made a total of seven men. Believe me, trying to make a party of seven men creep silently through the jungle is a nerve-wracking experience. Every twig that broke, or leaf that stirred, seemed like a gunshot.

The area that we were patrolling was not jungle in the true sense, it was more like woodland. For a few minutes we were creeping through trees, the next minute we came out into an open area with waist-high grass. As the leader of the patrol it was my job to ascertain the nature of the country ahead so that I could keep the patrol invisible if that was possible.

We were all well aware that the Japanese were doing exactly the same as us and at any moment we could have had a head-on confrontation with them. My orders were to patrol the woodlands area and to go as far as Admiralty Road. If we had neither seen nor engaged any Japanese we were to return to base. Finally, after what seemed like three hours, but was actually three-quarters of an hour, I sighted the main road and with a great feeling of relief decided that the mission was accomplished and it was time to turn back.

We started on the return journey, all of us breathing a little easier but still alert, knowing how cunning the Japs were. They could quite

51

easily have crept in behind and caught us on the return journey and either killed or captured us to stop us disclosing their whereabouts. Fortunately, we returned to our unit in safety and I was able to report that we had neither seen nor contacted any Japanese. On this information it was decided that my platoon would move through the woodlands area to guard Admiralty Road.

As a section commander I had been issued with a sub-machine gun; the rest had 303 Lee Enfield rifles. I decided to fire off a few shots into the trees and pressed the trigger of my gun. The only result was the dull plop of the bolt going forward and hitting the cartridge, no burst of fire came from the gun. I re-cocked the gun and pressed the trigger again with the same result – my Tommy gun was useless. If we had met up with any Japs I would have been defenceless – it was a horrifying thought.

I reported this to my platoon commander and we found out that some soldiers had been issued with Thompson sub-machine guns and others had been issued with Remington SMGs. One has a rim firing pin, the other a centre firing pin. I had been issued with the wrong ammunition. I was issued with the normal 303 rifle and ammunition, and my (toy) machine gun was withdrawn.

Shortly after this episode our company moved to the woodland area as reinforcements for the troops who were fighting in the Johor Straits area. Their job was to stop the Japanese crossing the Causeway. My Company Headquarters was situated in the Woodlands Golf Course clubhouse and our position gave us good views of the surrounding area. Straight ahead was a large area of trees and after we had heard the sounds of battle going on for some time word came through that some Japanese were amongst these trees. It was now even more obvious that they were across the Johor Straits and on the island.

Number Sixteen Platoon was ordered into action to attack the Japs in the wooded area. Then came the sounds of furious gunfire, which gradually subsided until all was quiet. There was no sign of any movement from either the Japs or from the men of Sixteen Platoon. Shortly after this orders came through that the rest of our company, Seventeen and Eighteen Platoons, were to move up to forward positions. Number Seventeen Platoon was ordered into action and my platoon was on stand-by as reserves. Now there were sounds of battle all around us and steadily getting closer. Suddenly, we were in the thick of it. The Japanese had broken through and we were being attacked. Orders came through that we were to take up a defensive position on the bank of a small river that the Japanese had yet to cross.

After a lull in the battle, the Japanese opened up again and mortars bombed our position. I stood up to change my position when I felt the blast of a mortar bomb on my body which knocked me off my feet. After a few moments I found that I was not wounded on the body but in my legs and shins. It was very painful. I retired to a safer position and when I examined my legs I could see blood on my puttees and socks. I quickly unwound my puttees and when I pulled down my socks I found both my legs in the shin area were peppered with stones and mud fragments. The force of the blast had sent the stones and grit right through all my clothes. I used my field dressing to bandage my legs as best I could, then I pulled up my socks and put my puttees on over the field dressing. The battle continued all around me.

Suddenly, all went quiet. We were ordered to withdraw and take up a defensive position on higher ground. This ground turned out to be a hillside cemetery that gave a good view of the surrounding countryside. My section was given a position where there were two or three freshly dug graves, still unoccupied. These made good trenches for my men. There was also an open-sided, tile-roofed building with a large marble-topped table in the centre, which I suppose was used for ceremonies. It was cool and shady, so I decided to use it as an observation post.

Although my section had not seen one Japanese soldier, suddenly we were under attack again. I was lying under the marble table firing at what I thought were Japs when suddenly I heard a crash above my head and then something landed on the table above me, hit the floor in front of me and rolled out of the building to the ground outside. It was an unexploded Japanese mortar bomb. Lucky break number two, but I was out of that building in a hell of a hurry.

We managed to hold off the Japanese and staged a counter-attack, once again taking up forward positions. This time our aim was to flush out those who had taken up a machine gun position in a house guarding a strategic road. It was our job to attack them. I was not happy. My legs were now painful and our ammunition was running low. For several days we had hardly had any food; all we had was what we could scrounge from empty houses.

My section took up a position facing the house occupied by the Japs. Unfortunately, we had no heavy weapons and would have to rely entirely on our 303 rifles. It was not a good prospect. Behind me and to my left was another road on which I could see one of our supply trucks standing unoccupied, obviously abandoned. It was no more than 25yds away and I was debating whether I would go and investigate what it contained when suddenly I saw a figure dash across the road towards the truck. Before he reached it there was a burst of machine gun fire. The man's chest turned a brilliant red and he fell face down in the road.

In those few brief moments I recognized him as a sergeant I had shared a cabin with on the USS *Wakefield*. He had taken a burst of fire full in the chest and must have died instantly. The firing from the Japanese was so accurate that they had the truck targeted to stop us getting near it. At the time this happened we were pinned down by the Japs. Owing to our shortage of ammunition we were loathe to use our Bren machine gun. Then word came through that we were to get some reinforcements.

I became aware of the noise of a vehicle behind me on the road. I turned around, fully expecting to see a Japanese truck or armoured car sneaking up on us, but I was amazed to see one of our own staff cars with our commanding officer standing up in it. With him was a small party of men. How they had been able to get along the road without being killed I will never know. On seeing me, the officer called out, 'Corporal, I want you to take charge of these men. They are Australians and have been separated from their unit.'

I carefully made my way across to them and asked if I should use the men with my section. The officer said, 'No.' I was to hand my section over to the next man in command (lance corporal) as he had another duty for the Australians and me. The officer then directed the six Australians and me to take up a defensive position in an empty house a few yards to the right of us. He also told us there were already two men in the house but he wanted it reinforced as he was sure the Japs were working their way around our right flank, which later proved true. The battle seemed to be going on all around us but not directly where we were.

At about 3.45pm things were getting quieter and by 4.00pm there was just an occasional rattle of machine gun fire or the sound of gunfire, and then it finally ceased altogether. My companions and I were at a loss to understand why this was happening. We didn't know what to do so we just kept our heads down and laid low. Of course, we were still very observant and expected at any moment a horde of Japs would come streaming down the road.

Finally, I saw one of my company men coming across the lawn of the house we were in. I called out to him from a window and he seemed most surprised to see me. I asked what was going on, and then it was my turn to be surprised when he told me the war was over. A ceasefire had taken effect at four o'clock in the afternoon, but all troops were to maintain their positions until further orders.

The house we had occupied was a two-storied house and we had gone straight upstairs to the front to command a view of the surrounding area. There were several other houses similar to the one we were in, but owing to the trees and shrubs in the gardens it was difficult to see clearly what they were like. As everything was quiet we decided to explore the house. The upstairs consisted of two large bedrooms and one smaller bedroom. There was a very large living room which opened out onto a balcony which overlooked a swimming pool. Also upstairs was a large bathroom and toilet. Judging by the state of the bedrooms it looked as though the place had been vacated in a great hurry.

Downstairs was a large reception hall with two rooms opening off each side; one appeared to be a library, the other an office. Walking through the hall, a door opened into what was obviously the servants' quarters. There was a large kitchen, which was a general living area, and one large and one small bedroom; also a shower and a squat lavatory. There was one more door which led out into a courtyard and underneath the house. This was the normal way of building in the tropics so as to get the maximum air circulation.

We were all very hungry and so the next thing was to examine the kitchen cupboards to see if there was any food. We found several unopened tins and shared the contents. Finally, we spread ourselves on beds around the house and had our first real sleep for days.

In the morning we had another scrounge around for food, but other than uncooked rice there was nothing else in the kitchen. We had a debate about what we should do. I was supposed to be in charge, but I was no match for six Australian soldiers and two men from another English regiment. The Aussies were all for leaving the house and going scrounging around the other houses to see what they could find. The two Englishmen wanted to find their unit. As for me, I didn't care about anything. I was just damned glad it was all over.

We heard a voice outside calling for us to show ourselves. We went outside to find an Australian sergeant with a group of other men, both British and Australian. He said he was rounding us up to rendezvous at a certain place to have a head count of survivors. We were marching along the road when suddenly we were surrounded by a group of Japanese soldiers. Up until this moment I had not seen a Jap at close quarters. They were very animated, pointing their rifles and, in some cases, bayonets at us. Although we couldn't understand their grunts and strange language, it was quite obvious they were telling us to hurry up. I was not at all sure what to do at that time and looked to the sergeant for a lead. He seemed quite calm and told us not to look frightened or act as though we were in a panic, but to just keep in a bunch and keep walking.

We rounded a bend on the road and to the left of us was a large open space which could have been a sports ground. In this area were a large number of soldiers and officers. Our sergeant led us up to an officer and after the usual saluting and reporting, left us with the remainder of the men who were already there. The Japanese soldiers who had joined us on the road were still standing around and talking among themselves.

On looking around I saw that the area was surrounded by Jap soldiers and soon a Japanese who was obviously an officer or a sergeant came over to our group. At the sight of his approach we all sprang to attention. Soon others were led away to join the rest of the Japanese, who were guarding us British and Australians.

I didn't recognize the British officer whom we had been left with. He took our names and numbers, also the names of our regiments. He then told us to go and pile our arms and ammunition in a large heap that was supervised by some Japanese soldiers. One of our party threw his rifle on the heap and it landed with a loud clatter. One of the Japs lunged towards the man and shouted at him. For a moment, I thought he was going to hit him. It was made quite plain that we were not to throw our weapons on the heap but to place them on carefully. After we had obeyed our officer's instructions he seemed to lose interest in us and so we mingled with the other men. I was hoping to meet up with one of my own men, or at least someone whom I would recognize, but had no such luck. I experienced a terrible sense of loneliness despite being surrounded by so many people.

My memories of that day are of feeling hungry and very tired. I suppose, like a lot of other men, I was quite shocked at what was happening to us. Fortunately, I kept my pack and other equipment, including my water bottle, so at least I had a change of clothing if I should need it and some drinking water.

I found a comparatively quiet place and, using my pack for a pillow, went to sleep. How long I slept I have no idea, but I awoke to hear a lot of shouting going on and someone telling me to get up as we were moving off. I managed to get up and put my pack on, but my head was aching terribly and I felt quite ill. From that time on all I have are shadowy memories of walking along a road with a lot of men around me and an awful lot of noise. The heat was intolerable and I had visions of throwing my pack away and even, at times, getting undressed. At last we stopped and, again, I had vague memories of being helped to walk.

When I later became aware of things going on around me, it was to find myself lying on the floor wrapped in a blanket. There was a group of men sitting around talking. One got up and came to me and asked how I felt. I asked him where I was and he told me I was at Changi. I managed to sit up and look around. It seemed that I was in a kind of large stone hall with a concrete floor, full of men's belongings. He said that he and the other men thought I had some sort of fever. I had been in and out of consciousness for about two days.

It is rather a strange thing that I have no real recollection of the period immediately after the surrender. Obviously I must have been fed and watered and carried on a fairly normal life. I remember attending an open air church service to honour our dead and the chaplain thanking God for our survival. I did wonder then what the future held for us and how long we would continue to survive.

I have read different accounts of the events after the surrender, and seen photographs of all the prisoners being forced to line the route with their backs turned as the Japanese high command drove by reviewing their success in capturing Singapore. I can't even recall taking part in that episode. I have a feeling that this incident happened about two weeks after I reached Changi.

I have clear recollections of later events. The Japanese more or less left us to our own devices and we were free to wander around the area we were in. I found that I was able to go to a beach by crossing some village grounds. There did not appear to be anyone around at that time. I noticed a hut that stood on the boundary of a large white house. On occasions, I thought I had seen someone in the hut, but had not had the nerve to go near it. One day I saw an old man outside the hut with his back to me and so I went over to speak to him. I found he was Chinese. At first he was frightened, but after a few moments he relaxed. He asked me if I would drink tea with him. He spoke reasonably good English and told me how upset he and his daughter were about the English losing Singapore.

I did not go that way for a couple of days but when I did I decided to have another chat with him. I went to the hut but it was empty. I was going to continue my journey to the beach when the old man appeared from around the back of the hut. I greeted him and asked if he was alright. He said something that I couldn't understand and took me around to the back of the hut. He showed me how the Japanese had put a thick barbed wire fence between his hut and the house. He again offered me tea and told me that the hut he was living in was just an old shed that belonged to the big house. He had been an employee, as had his wife. His daughter was just about to leave school when Singapore fell.

The Japanese had taken over the house. They had kept his wife to work for them and made him go and live on his own. He had not seen his daughter for a few days and was very worried about both of them. I felt very sorry for him. A day or so after this meeting I started out for the beach and found that the Japs had put barbed wire close to our building, so we were now prisoners.

It was shortly after this episode that an officer visited us and said that the Japanese had asked if some of the British POWs wanted to go into Singapore city and assist the civilians in cleaning up the war damage. They said they were only interested in men who had experience in the trades, such as plumbing or carpentry. The officer was rather negative about the idea and said that the Japanese had made the mess and they should be left to clean it up. He suggested we should say we were all clerks or non-skilled men but he would come back later and take our names if we wanted to go. Later that day we were paid a visit by another officer. He was accompanied by a Japanese who spoke to us in their language while the officer interpreted for our benefit. He said that if we wanted to work for the Japanese Imperial Army in Singapore we would be well treated and would have better food. Our own officers would be in charge of us and we would not be ill-treated if we worked hard. The British officer would take our names and any trade skills we had and the Japanese would select those they required. The outcome of this was that all of our group were skilled men, one saying he was a glass polisher. Later we asked what that was and he said, 'A window cleaner. It sounds more important, right?' We had to agree. I put myself down as a woodworker.

The next day we were all inspected by the Japanese. This was the first time that men from different parts of the camp had been together. For the first time I saw someone I recognized as belonging to my Company. He was a sergeant from Company HQ. As soon as I was able to break away from my group without the Japanese noticing, I made myself known to him. He was as surprised as I was when we met and we had time to catch up. He told me that near the end of hostilities my platoon had been ordered to attack a Japanese machine gun nest. My platoon had gone into the attack but, unknown to them, there had been another machine gun strong point only a short distance away and they had been caught in murderous crossfire. Nearly all were killed or wounded. Just before we parted company he said, 'By the way, you are about the only NCO left in your platoon and you're now a sergeant. You've been promoted on the field of battle.' At the time I thought, 'That's a fat lot of good now. I should have had the promotion before the battle, not after it.'

The next morning we were woken by the Japanese guards yelling at us to get up. We were outside on parade for a roll call as dawn was breaking. Each of us was issued with a parcel of food and told that it contained our day's rations. I was expecting to see a convoy of trucks arrive to take us to Singapore city but that was naive of me. The Japs had learnt a couple of English words. The most frequently heard were, 'Hurry up', or, as they said it, 'Hurrup', and the other detested word was, 'Speedo'. So, to many shouts of these two words, we moved off. Once we were on the move I resolved to try to speak to my sergeant again.

The other men seemed to know more than I did. One of them said it was about fifteen 'bloody' miles to Singapore from Changi. We started off marching in an orderly manner but as time went on and the day got hotter we became more and more like a disorderly rabble. Fortunately, the Japs allowed us a few minutes break every hour or so, more for their own benefit than ours, I suspect. It was during the first break that my friend and I spotted each other. On the next stage of the journey we were able to walk together as by this time the Japs were not bothered by who was with whom as long as we kept moving.

After chatting for a short time my friend said, 'Here, you'd better put this on,' and passed me an armband with three stripes on it. He then told me that he had a couple of spare ones and he wouldn't miss the one he had passed to me. He thought the Japanese might take more notice of three stripes than two. So, with no further ado, I quietly slipped it onto my arm.

I then asked him if he knew what had happened to our kitbags. When we had gone into action we had only been allowed to dress in battle order which meant that our backpacks contained the bare necessities of life such as spare socks, spare clothing and underwear. Our other heavier and personal gear had been left back at Company HQ. I had been hoping all along that I would be able to claim my kitbag as there was so much in it that I needed. Spare boots, blankets, cigarettes, presents and souvenirs, as well as some money; in fact, all my personal belongings.

His reply astonished me. He told me that after the surrender all our kitbags, and a lot of other gear, had been put into a great pile, doused with petrol and burnt, so that the Japanese wouldn't get at our belongings. That was a terrible thing to hear when my spirits were at such a low ebb. I really felt I had lost everything. All I had left was what I stood up in and what was on my back.

As the day got hotter our march turned into the usual nightmare of exhaustion, sweat and the effort of putting one foot in front of the other. The Japanese told us that if any men fell by the wayside they would be returned to Changi so, of course, we all tried desperately hard to keep going.

At last we saw houses on the outskirts of the city and we came to an area surrounded by barbed wire. A wooden gate was opened for us to enter the enclosure and the guards motioned us to form lines, four or five deep. Although we were tired and exhausted with standing in the hot sun, it was a relief just to be able to stand still and not to have to keep on walking.

Chapter 11

River Valley Camp

After a very short wait, a car drove in through the gates and we could see by the attitude of the guards that this person was going to be a 'Number One'. I had already learned from the Japanese that anyone of rank was always referred to in English as 'Number One'. When he stepped out of the car there was a lot of bowing and many commands were given. As he approached, we automatically stood to attention. It was quite obvious he intended to inspect us. After he had finished, the car drove over to near where we were and the driver produced a small platform. The officer stepped on to it and proceeded to speak to us, in surprisingly good English. He more or less repeated what we had been told by our own officer before we left Changi. He said that we would be working for the Japanese Emperor and that if we worked hard we would be well fed and treated. When he had departed the Japanese split us up into groups and took us to the huts. They made us understand that these huts were to be our home.

The huts followed a similar pattern to others we had seen. They were built to hold about forty men. There was a central aisle with a raised platform on both sides, where we were to sleep and live. On either side of the aisle was a row of poles about 7ft apart, pre-sumably to support the roof. Also, they formed a division to the platform. As we passed through the hut the guard pointed out that two men would occupy each of the spaces between the poles. When we realized this a bit of jostling went on so that you didn't get stuck with someone you couldn't stand the sight of. It is quite well known that great friendships can be built up in close proximity, but also great hatreds. When it came to my turn, the guard, pointing to the armband I was wearing, said something I couldn't understand. I then learnt I was to have a space to myself.

After we had settled ourselves in, a call came to parade outside again because it was mealtime. Although the Japs supplied our food rations, they were supervised, cooked and distributed by our own cooks. We queued up for our ration and got something better than at Changi. Later I heard that the Japanese had sent an advance party to the camp to prepare for our arrival.

The platform we were to live on was made of wooden boards. After sleeping on a concrete floor with only one blanket, the wooden floor felt almost soft. At the very least it was a lot warmer. In the morning the Japs woke us up by yelling and shouting at us, not that it was much different to what we had been accustomed to from our own NCOs. I had done my share of making a nuisance of myself in order to wake men up at reveille. After we had washed and had the usual breakfast of rice, we were paraded outside the huts and roll call was taken. We knew by their behaviour that something important was to happen.

The same car we had seen the previous day drove into the compound. After stopping, the driver opened the door and an English-speaking Japanese officer got out, accompanied by a British and an Australian officer. I noticed that there seemed to be more Japanese soldiers around than there were the previous day. The officer gave a long speech, more or less repeating what he had said the day before, but adding the fact that although the camp would be under a Japanese commander, camp discipline would be maintained by our own officers. When he had finished speaking there was another stir among the Japanese and, with the usual ceremony, a new officer was introduced to us as the Camp Commandant. He spoke to us through a Japanese interpreter and told us that we must learn some Japanese words of command. His orders were to be demonstrated by a group of Japanese soldiers. We were to repeat the words each time they were spoken.

Our first lesson was to learn numbers, and so we began: *Ichi* – one, *Ni* – two, *San* – three, *Shi* – four, *Go* – five, *Roku* – six, *Shichi* – seven, *Hachi* – eight, *Ku* – nine, *Ju* – ten. On reaching *Ju* (or ten) the next numbers become *Ju ichi, Ju ni, Ju san* or, as we would say, ten one, ten two, ten three, or ten, eleven, twelve and thirteen respectively. *Ni ichi* and *Ni san*, were twenty-one and twenty-two. On reaching one hundred the word is *Akka*. Later, we were given numbers to work out among ourselves. *Roku akka ju go* is six hundred and fifteen.

Each time a command was given the group of soldiers would demonstrate it and we would have to follow their actions while at the same time, calling out the words. The first word was *Joskay*: attention. We had to practice this umpteen times, of course, before our tormentor was satisfied. *Hedari* meant left and *migi* meant right, and so on.

Finally, our ordeal was over and we were directed back to our huts. Shortly after we had settled down, some soldiers came into the huts and began to sort us into groups of about eight men, each group having one NCO in it. When my turn came to be chosen, I was *Ichi*, the rest were *Ni, San, Shi, Go, Roku, Shichi* and *Hachi*. The soldier pointed to my armband and said, 'Ichi, you Number One.' So I was in charge of our group.

Once we had been sorted out, our own officer came into the hut and told us that he had been chosen as Liaison Officer because he was able to speak Japanese. He was responsible for our discipline and general behaviour. The Japanese who had sorted us into groups were the guards in charge of the working parties. They would come the following morning to collect us for our jobs.

Morning came and we all wondered what was in store. When the guards arrived, my guard came to me and in quite good English said, 'I am the guard of you. My name is Nakazawa.' He handed me a piece of paper with his name written on it: NAKAZAWA. I thanked him politely and said his name. He said it was OK and then, pointing to my stripes, told me that the word for sergeant was *Gunso*, then asked my name. I told him, 'Jackson.' He looked at me for a moment and then asked me again for my name and I repeated, 'Jackson.' When I repeated my name he called out to another soldier and asked him to come over to where we were standing. I was a little apprehensive as to why he was calling his colleague over to us. Pointing to my armband he called out, 'Him English soldier, *Gunso* Injection.' He made a pretence of injecting himself in the arm and both seemed to think it was quite a joke. As for me, I was very relieved to see them laughing and so, from that day on, I remained '*Gunso* Injection.'

Nakazawa then led our party out of the camp and on to the road. As we walked along the road I couldn't help thinking how ridiculous we must look. We were supposed to be proud British soldiers, the guardians of Singapore. Yet, here we were, a motley ill-dressed gang in the charge of one small soldier whose rifle and bayonet were nearly as big as he was. I am sure we could quite easily have overpowered him and made our escape, but we were all well aware that there was nowhere to escape to.

We had not gone far when Nakazawa stopped at a large house and motioned us to go in through a big entrance gate. In front of the house was a large lawn with several soldiers standing around. Upon our entrance, one of them came over to us and Nakazawa, bowing to him in the usual way, spoke to him in Japanese. After telling him I was Gunso Injection, accompanied by the usual laughter, he left us in the man's care. Our new boss didn't give his name, just said, 'Me, Number One', and so that is how I addressed him, and I was 'Injection'.

Number One led us across the lawn to where an area had been roped off. By sign language he made us understand we were to build something there. He then went to a satchel on a small table and produced a couple of drawings to show me. Fortunately, it looked to be a fairly simple structure consisting of a roof supported by a number of upright poles. The roof appeared to be iron and the walls were palm leaf thatch. As we looked at it he was jabbering away and pointing at the drawing. Every few seconds he would look at me and say, 'OK?'

We managed to establish some sort of rapport and it seemed the first task was to dig about a dozen holes for the posts to be sunk into the ground. We were issued with the necessary tools and he pointed out where the first hole was to be dug. I made my way to where he was pointing with a shovel in my hand but, saying something in his own language, he motioned me to put it down and made one of the other men pick it up and start digging.

Reaching into his satchel he produced a measuring tape and made me understand that I was to help him measure up the ground. I was holding the tape and now and again he would call out something to me. I couldn't understand so made no answer. I could see he was getting quite exasperated and finally, laying the tape on the ground, he came and grabbed my arm and shouted, 'Ichi Ni San Shi Go,' and pointed to the tape. I understood then that he had been calling out numbers, so I said, 'OK.' I also realized that the measurements on the tape were not in feet and inches but in metres and centimetres. What he had been calling out were such things as, 'Ni metre

Go centimetre,' or in English, 2m and 5cm. Once I got the hang of the measuring system I was able to understand what he wanted and translate it for my men.

Fortunately, my training in carpentry and joinery stood me in good stead. When the time came to start the timber construction I made quite a good job of the joints we needed. We learnt from him that the house was to be occupied by some high ranking officers and that we were building a cookhouse for the guards who would be on duty day and night, patrolling the grounds.

Nakazawa took us to the job each morning and came again at about five o'clock to take us back to the camp. While we were travelling we used to talk to each other. It was surprising how much English he could speak. One question I asked him was why he likened my name to the word 'injection'. He told me that he had started on a course as a medical student where there had been some English-speaking doctors, but he had been called up before he could finish his studies. He taught me a few words of Japanese, which was becoming more and more necessary. I in turn taught him some words of English. Although he didn't smoke he would often pass me a couple of cigarettes saying, 'My friends give to me, I give to you.' I was very grateful for his kindness.

Number One, who was in charge of the building programme, was neither friendly nor unfriendly. He allowed us quite a few breaks during the day and certainly made no attempt to ill-treat us. We finally nailed the roof on the building and he told us that some local Chinese would be coming to add the palm leaf thatch to the walls.

From this experience I learnt that my sergeant stripes were beneficial as they saved me from some hard work. Shortly after we had finished our cookhouse job, Nakazawa took us to a row of small bungalows on the outskirts of the city. I am not sure who occupied them but it looked as though they had been built for semi-military personnel. The bungalows had been damaged, probably by vandals. There were lots of smashed windows and broken glass and doors with holes kicked in them.

Nakazawa assigned each man a bungalow and told them to clean it up. My bungalow consisted of a combined kitchen and living room, a small bedroom, a toilet and a bathroom with a shower. The bedroom had a built-in wardrobe and tallboy, as well as a dressing-table set in a recess. The general state of the place was not too bad

65

and I soon had it tidy. I decided to be nosey and look in the cupboards, not expecting to find anything as most places had been ransacked by now. When I opened the wardrobe doors my heart nearly skipped a beat. Hanging there were two nice clean khaki shirts. The next thing was to look in the drawers of the tallboy. When I found two pairs of shorts, I thought that I was having a wonderful dream. Add to this a couple of pairs of socks and a pair of sandals. It was a complete wardrobe for me.

Of course, the questions arose: would they be missed if I took them and would they fit me and lastly, how would I get them back to the camp? Fortunately, I always carried my water bottle and haversack with me whenever I went out on a job. I rolled all the clothing up as tight and as small as I could and put them in the haversack. The socks I stuffed into my pockets and the sandals I wrapped in an old towel that I found in the bathroom. All the time I was afraid that Nakazawa would come in to see how I was getting on with the clean-up. Luckily he did not come in but called me out. I went outside carrying my bag in my hand with the rolled up towel stuffed in the top. Nakazawa examined the bungalows and seemed satisfied with what we had done.

After I had washed and had a meal I couldn't wait to try on my new clothes. The shirts and shorts were both a bit on the large side but quite wearable, better that than too small. The socks, too, were a comfortable fit but the sandals were rather tight. After a time, though, they became more comfortable. For a few days I was worried about what I had done but I heard no more about it so began to enjoy my new-found elegance.

To say that my gang and I had made friends with Nakazawa would be stretching things. He seemed to enjoy practising English with us and taught us some essential Japanese phrases. As long as we did our work he seemed quite amenable.

One day we were taken to a stone building that had a long wooden verandah, roofed over with tiles. The house was in good order, but the verandah had been badly damaged, with broken wood and tiles everywhere. It was our job to clean it up. The veranda was about 0.5m high from the ground and about 15m long, with steps up to it at the right-hand end. None of us bothered walking backwards and forwards to the steps, we just stepped up or down off it wherever we happened to be.

On this particular day I had decided to wear my sandals because my boots were getting rather badly worn. I stepped backwards off the veranda and felt a terrible pain in my foot. When I looked to see what had happened I found I had stepped on to a piece of wood with a long nail standing up from it. It had gone through the sole of my sandal and also through my foot. I could actually see the nail sticking up between the bones of the second and third toes of my right foot. I shouted out for someone to help me and a couple of the boys came, as did Nakazawa. He directed operations, standing on the board while my two mates just lifted me off it. The wound started to bleed quite badly and we had nothing to dress it with. Nakazawa said he would take me to a Japanese Army doctor who lived nearby if all the men would promise to do 'good work' while he was away.

After a quick consultation between the doctor and Nakazawa the doctor cleaned up my bloody foot and, using a small brush, painted in and around the wound with iodine, which was very painful. While this was going on I could hear Nakazawa saying, '*Jhoto Nie,*' which was Japanese for 'no good,' and when I turned to look at him I saw tears in his eyes. After the doctor had bound up my foot I heard Nakazawa telling him the usual story about my name being Injection. The doctor thought it was quite a joke and so we parted on good terms.

When we returned to my group Nakazawa told me not to work and the next day I was to rest. The next morning he arrived at the camp and came straight to where I slept. He handed me a small parcel and indicated I was not to open it until he and the working party had gone. When I opened the parcel I found a tin of condensed milk, a small loaf of bread and a packet of cigarettes, plus a note which I kept for years.

I am sorry for your hurt, you good English soldier. I like you. For two days you rest. I give you small gift help you get good quick.
    The guard of you Nakazawa

He came in the evening to see how I was feeling and I wanted to thank him for his gift and note. He must have read my mind and motioned me to not say anything. I held out my hand to him and we just shook hands very firmly. I could sense he was embarrassed.

When I got back to work I mentioned about the note and remarked on his English. He told me he didn't write it himself, but a friend of his spoke 'good English' and had written it for him.

One morning Nakazawa came to take us out to work. When we arrived at the job he told us that he was being moved and tomorrow we would have a new guard. This came as quite a shock to all of us as we liked talking to Nakazawa. He had taught us several Japanese phrases. Many of our conversations were a mixture of our bad Japanese and his limited English, but we seemed to understand each other.

We wondered what our new guard would be like. Each one had their own personality: some were noisy, shouting things like, 'speedo, speedo,' and, 'hurrup, hurrup', others were quietly contemptuous, as though we were just a nuisance to them.

When the guards arrived there seemed to be a little more noise than usual. Our new one came into the hut shouting at the top of his voice. At first we couldn't make out what he was yelling, but as he got closer I heard, 'Joskay Injection.' Translated this meant, 'Attention, Jackson,' so obviously he was looking for me. When I realized this I stepped forward and said something like, 'Are you looking for me, mate?' In reply, I got a torrent of Japanese and some threatening gestures with his rifle, which didn't bode well for the future. This guard was short, thick-set, and not much taller than 5ft. With close-cropped hair, his features were almost monkey-like. The most noticeable thing about him, when he opened his mouth, was the number of gold teeth he had top and bottom. He looked and sounded so repulsive we later nicknamed him 'Satan'.

Satan took us back to where we had first gone to build the cook-house. He could speak no English, so when we arrived at the job he reported to a Japanese officer and he came and spoke to us. By means of his limited English and my even more limited Japanese, we learnt we were to build a similar building. This was because a lot more men were arriving and it was to be for them to eat in; in other words, a mess room. I asked the officer if the man I had worked with on the original hut was going to be in charge. He made me understand that the man had gone away and I was to be in charge of the gang with regards to the building. Satan was to have charge of the tools and equipment, which were kept locked in a small outhouse at the side of the main building. All through this explanation, Satan was interrupting and jabbering away like a monkey.

We went to the shed and drew what tools we needed and began our task.

Eventually a couple of holes appeared which seemed to please Satan. Up until this time he had been jabbering away in Japanese and getting quite excited. Had he had his way we would have dug holes all over the place.

At lunchtime we were chatting amongst ourselves when Satan butted in. He seemed to be interested in what we were eating. He wasn't impressed and said, '*Jhoto Nie*' (no good), and showed us his food. He had what looked like a large omelette and quite a big tin of rice. Of course, we all nodded approval and he seemed quite pleased. He ate the omelette with obvious relish and then he did an amazing thing. He pointed to my mess tin and motioned that he wanted to give me some rice. I couldn't believe that such an evil looking man wanted to give his food away. I held out my mess tin and he pushed some rice into it with his chopsticks and then went to each of us sharing it out as evenly as he could.

The next morning Satan was a little quieter but was still making himself heard. Off we went to the job and after drawing our tools, started work. About the middle of the morning Satan called for us to stop work and rest. He took me round the side of the house and showed me a large wok of tea (*aucha*) simmering over a charcoal fire. He gave me to understand that provided we asked his permission we could drink some during our breaks. The tea, or *aucha* as the Japs call it, is just water that is kept simmering, and every now and again one of the guards throws in a handful of tea. It is never allowed to boil or get too strong and we found it most refreshing. After a short break we started work again until finally the signal came for our lunch break. We ate our ration of rice more or less in silence. Satan looked almost as though he had dozed off. We also lounged around looking quite relaxed.

Suddenly, Satan jumped to his feet and started pointing at us and shouting, '*Speedo, speedo*, hurrup, hurrup,' and generally going barmy. We all jumped to our feet and started work, wondering what all the fuss was about. All became clear when we saw a Japanese officer approaching. Poor old Satan was only showing his authority. We carried on with our work as it always paid to be very busy when an officer appeared on the scene. If the officer didn't think we were working hard enough he would take his anger out on the guard and the guard would then take his resentment out on his gang of

69

prisoners. We had no wish for this to happen with someone as unpredictable as Satan.

After the usual ceremonial bowing, Satan and the officer looked at what we had done. They spoke only in Japanese, so we had no idea what this visit was about. When the officer left the site I fully expected Satan to start shouting at us or showing some sort of displeasure, but he must have been quite satisfied with us as we were left to carry on as usual.

We were coming to the end of the job and somehow we had also come to an understanding with Satan. Providing we showed him some respect and did our work he seemed quite a reasonable bloke (in spite of his appearance). Funnily enough, after a time he began to look quite normal.

One evening I was quite surprised to see Satan coming into our hut. This was most unusual as the work guards never came near us except at work parties. He came to me and motioned for us to go outside. I was worried about what he wanted me for, and so were my mates. The Japanese were often unpredictable.

We prisoners had made some seats out of odds and ends and Satan motioned for us to sit down on one. We sat down and the first thing he did was to offer me an English cigarette. I was very surprised. After we lit up he reached inside his shirt and produced a photo of himself (at least I assumed it was he, because he looked quite different in the photograph) with a woman and two children. He then confirmed my assumption by pointing to the photo and then to himself. As he pointed to each person in turn he said, 'English Nah.' He wanted me to teach him the English words for each of his family. As I taught him the meaning of 'wife', 'son', daughter', 'you', 'me', and a number of other words, I began to realise that he was picking up the words with a London accent. While I was teaching him, he also taught me a little Japanese.

He asked me about my wife and if I had any children. Fortunately, one of the few personal things I had been able to save was a photograph of my wife and son. I got it from my pack and showed it to him. For a short time I think we felt sorry for each other. About an hour and two cigarettes later it had got dark, so he left me.

The next morning when we had our break for *aucha* he surprised us all by passing round a packet of cigarettes saying, 'Cigaretto good.' He waited for us to light up and then said all sorts of odd things like, 'You, me, him, her.' He looked very pleased when we said, 'OK, very good Number One, English *Jhoto*' (good).

Satan came to visit me on two other nights and we talked to each other as best we could. Of course, my gang were quite happy because the next day we always got a fag or two. If we could keep him talking we got an extra long break from work.

Finally, the job was finished. We wondered what awaited us next.

Chapter 12

The Bridge

Satan arrived as usual the next morning, but instead of leaving the camp he took us across it to the other side, adjacent to the river. When we arrived we found quite a large gathering of other prisoners and guards. I saw an acquaintance and asked him if he knew what was going to happen. He said he had heard a rumour that we were going to build a bridge.

For a short time we just stood around chatting with one another. The guard didn't seem too concerned about us. Then someone said, 'Hey lads, look at this lot.' Coming around a bend in the river were two barges loaded with timber. They pulled in to the river bank. It was obviously going to be our job to unload all the timber. I was waiting for the Japs to tell us what to do, when I heard an unmistakably English voice shouting, 'Righto you lot, come on, get these barges unloaded.' The voice belonged to a British senior sergeant. At that moment I realized that my sergeant's stripes weren't going to mean much on this job.

While we were unloading the barges I learnt that the bridge we were going to build would be across the Singapore River. Our POW camp was on one side of the river and the Japanese lived on the other side. To get to and from our camp was a considerable walk to the nearest available bridge and, at times, we had to carry some quite heavy equipment.

The timber was extremely heavy, very long and soaking wet. Most of the time we were up to our waists in the cold water. Added to this, having to hear the grating voice of the sergeant all day made it a miserable experience.

The next day Satan took us back to the bridge site. We had unloaded most of the timber the previous day, so that was one blessing. Later in the morning I saw 'Righto, you lot' talking to a Japanese soldier. As they came nearer I recognised the Jap as

'Number One', the boss from my first job building the cookhouse. They walked past me and I saw Number One looking at me as I was lifting some quite heavy timber. I looked directly at him. They passed on and, standing by the riverbank, had a discussion about the proposed bridge. They were there for some time and I was still lugging lumps of wood around. Finally, they turned round and came towards me. Number One stopped and said to me, 'You, nameo.' I told him Jackson and he immediately said, 'Injection'. I replied, 'You Number One, OK?' He laughed and went off with the sergeant.

A little while later the sergeant came to me and asked how I knew Number One. So I told him of my experience building the cook-house. He then told me that as a regular soldier he had been stationed in Singapore for some time. He had been friends with some Japanese people and learnt their language, which was why he had been put in charge of us. Number One was, of course, going to be overall boss as architect of the bridge. Our guards would still make sure we behaved ourselves, and 'Sarge', as he became to all and sundry, was to give the orders.

After the episode with Number One my life became a bit easier. There was a lot of digging to be done before any actual construction work was started, but I was spared that. Also, when heavy timber was to be moved, I found that there were plenty of helpers. Both Sarge and Number One used me quite frequently to help them when any measuring was necessary. The whole bridge was to be timber and entailed a lot of hand sawing of quite large logs.

We had two gangs working, one on each side of the river. The plan was that eventually the bridge builders would meet up in the centre of the river. Once work on the riverbanks had been completed it was time to move onto the actual bridge construction. The 'powers that be' had decided the best way to approach the job was to use two large boats for us to stand on while we worked. We were to cut large pieces of timber and float them into whatever position was needed. We had cut several small pieces and the idea worked well. It then became necessary to cut a very large piece. It took quite a long time to cut it as it was also very hard wood. Finally, we finished cutting it and it dropped into the river with a mighty splash. It immediately disappeared below the surface and we all waited for it to reappear. We waited in vain and it became obvious that the wood was so heavy it had sunk for good. The Japanese guard in charge of our party was very angry. We couldn't understand what he was shouting but it was quite obvious he blamed us for losing the timber. Number One heard the commotion and came to see what had happened. The guard tried to get Number One to order us to dive into the river and rescue the wood. Common sense prevailed, however, and we managed to retrieve it with some grappling hooks.

For some reason the team on my side of the river had gotten ahead of the other team. Our part of the bridge was cantilevered out quite a long way from the bank. The Japanese thought it needed some support. Sarge suggested that we put a couple of props under it, sunk into the riverbed. The Japs decided a better idea was to anchor our boat under the bridge and prop it up with the board, which we duly did. We then went back to our huts, and the Japanese home to their quarters for the night.

The next morning our guards came to collect us to take us to the bridge. And as we came near the site we heard raised voices. The nearer we got the more obvious it became that something was wrong. We found our boat lying on the riverbed full of water. Of course, we thought it was a great joke but none of us even dared to smile. We had learnt that the Japanese sense of humour was strictly one-sided – their side.

What had happened was that the tide had risen overnight. The barge had tried to float on the tide but had been held in place by the bridge props. It had been a trial of strength between our bridge and the boat. The boat had been heavily laden with timber, so it didn't take much pressure from the bridge to sink it. Had the boat not sunk it could have torn the bridge completely away from the river-bank and all our work would have been wasted. Finally, when the Japs had all finished blaming themselves and Sarge for forgetting that the river was tidal, the boat was pumped out and we continued with our work. Much to the joy of the Japanese soldiers we finally finished the bridge.

Shortly after this we lost Satan; he just disappeared. He was there one day and gone the next. One morning, when we were waiting for him to take us to work, the 'Jockey' turned up instead. He looked just like one with his bowlegs, small and of slight build, which was topped off with a small jockey cap. He took us to one of our worst jobs. We were told we were going to a warehouse to clear up a mess. This was an understatement, for as soon as the door was opened the stench knocked us back. When we got inside we found out why.

Strewn around the place were crates and cases of tinned food. Corned beef, tongues, fruit, peas, you name it, it was all there. The tragedy was that every case had been smashed open by some means, and every tin deliberately damaged. Jockey made us understand that a truck would shortly be arriving and it was our job to load it with the stuff to be dumped. In the meantime, we were to pile it up near the entrance. Our only tools were a couple of shovels and our bare hands.

The warehouse had been closed up for weeks and as the temperature in Singapore was about 90° Fahrenheit, the food was putrid and there was a plague of flies. As we were carrying the boxes and crates to heaps near the door it became apparent that, despite the damage, some cans could still be salvaged. I had no idea of Jockey's temperament. So far we had only communicated in grunts, our limited Japanese, and sign language. He certainly didn't appear to be amiable. A couple of the lads decided to take a risk and if anything sound was found, placed it in a small pile separate from the rubbish. It gradually increased in size until there was enough to fill perhaps a tea chest. The Jockey had been hanging about outside most of the time. At last we heard the sound of a truck coming and so the Jockey opened the large front sliding doors. He inspected what we had done and spotted the pile of good tins. Pointing to the good pile he flew into a torrent of Japanese. Using his rifle butt and his feet he pushed and kicked all of them into the damaged pile. He was making it quite plain that we were to have none of it.

I was not aware at this time that the British powers had thought a scorched earth policy was a good idea, hence the destruction of our kitbags and now the destruction of food stocks. It appeared that this was done in several stores and warehouses to stop any of it falling into Japanese hands. As prisoners we were dependent on the Japanese for everything. We were now living on a diet of rice and vegetables because some stupid fools had decided to destroy our food stocks. Even worse than this was the fact that the warehouse next door contained hundreds of 20l (4gal) tins of aviation fuel for aircraft. These had been left intact and our lads were slaving away loading them aboard Japanese ships to be used in their war effort. Add to this hundreds of bags of cement and many, many other useful things that were being loaded. It was no wonder we felt sad. It took us a couple of days to clear up the warehouse (*godown*). We were really glad to see that job finished.

The men in the River Valley camp were a mixture of different British regiments and companies. There were also a number of Australians.

I was one of the few men whose kitbag had been burnt, which left me completely skint. A lot of the other men still had many of their personal possessions, such as clothes, boots and, perhaps, souvenirs bought on the way to Singapore. Others had watches, rings and, most importantly, money. If you had money it was possible to buy food from the Singaporeans. A lot of selling was done at night through the perimeter fence. It was a risky business because if you were caught by the guards both the buyer and the seller were beaten.

When money ran out there were ways of earning it. You could sell your possessions to the Singaporeans or the Japanese. The phrase, 'It's not worth a tin of fish,' was certainly not true in our case. There were many men who swapped a valuable item for a tin of herrings in tomato sauce.

When we first arrived at River Valley the Japanese had been true to their word and fed us quite well, but as time went on our rations got less and less. I lost quite a lot of weight and was quickly exhausted by the hard work expected from us. It was possible to report sick but not advisable, as the Japanese practice was that no work was rewarded by no food. If you finished up in the hospital hut you were put onto half rations and so we tried our best to keep working.

The Japanese officers thought they should punish people publicly. This was a lesson to the rest of us to behave ourselves. The usual procedure was for all of us to be paraded before or after work. The offender was then brought out in front of us and given a tirade of abuse by an officer, intermingled with slaps and punches. In some cases the culprit was hit with the officer's sheathed sword. I suppose the only defence one can offer for this inhumane treatment is that we actually saw Jap soldiers receiving the same punishment for their own misdemeanours.

On the lighter side, the Australians were segregated from the Brits inasmuch as they had their own huts, but we were allowed to visit each other and to mingle freely. Somehow the Aussies won permission to start a concert party. The Japanese even allowed them to use a spare hut as a theatre. The concert party built a stage and made quite a good job of a makeshift theatre, installing footlights and a spotlight. In all probability, had the British officers asked permission to start a concert party and the facilities to stage them, they would have been refused. The Japanese had more empathy with the Australians than with the British soldiers.

The actors and 'actresses' were drawn from the camp – anyone who showed any talent. Eventually a group was chosen. To us prisoners their shows were fantastic. We not only had comedians, jugglers, a fire eater, whistlers and many singers, we also had a small band. The star of the show was 'Judy Garland' – a most believable Judy. As a matter of fact she (he) was to become known to all of us as Judy. There were plenty of rumours about Judy, but there were also lots of rumours about the 'Andrews Sisters' (brothers). I think that in the end the concert party didn't know 'he' from 'she'.

Seating at the concerts was very limited so it was mostly restricted to VIPs, such as our own officers, and quite often we were honoured by visits from Japanese officers. The ordinary soldiers like myself had to stand and as many as possible squeezed in to see the show. Sometimes guards also came along and it was prudent to let them stand near the front. We would try to stand near or next to one of them because if they pulled out a packet of cigarettes there was a good chance of being offered one.

The comedians chose their jokes carefully, depending on the audience. We found out to our own detriment that it was very easy to offend the Japanese and none of us wanted the concert party shut down. Unfortunately, the lack of proper food and sickness took its toll and in the end the concert party gradually folded.

When we were out on our working parties we began to see more and more Indian soldiers. They marched with heads up, chests out, arms swinging. Each time we saw them we knew the Indian Army had turned themselves over to the Japanese.

At this time most of the work my group and I were doing was loading trucks with goods from *godowns* (warehouses). The trucks were taking the goods to the docks to be loaded onto ships. The Japanese were literally ransacking the island.

We prisoners had no reliable news source. Rumours abounded, mostly started by the Singaporeans. The Japanese were always telling us that they were winning the war, that England had been conquered by the Germans, and that we would have to spend the rest of our lives working for them. Of course, we tried to be sceptical and keep up our spirits but most of the time we were pretty miserable.

One morning no guards came to collect us. We hung around until late in the morning and finally one of the British camp officers told us that the Japanese soldiers had been called away and the camp was now in the hands of the Indian soldiers. Sure enough, when I looked around at the perimeter fence and the main gate, the guards were Indian. We assumed that there were to be no working parties.

The only means of cooking or heating was by burning wood. This meant that an endless supply had to be brought in to the camp. This was done by trailer parties. The trailer was a stripped down army flat-deck truck. The cab and all working parts had been removed so that all that was left were the wheels and chassis; this in itself was very heavy. Each day a gang of twenty or so men were detailed to pull this trailer and go out with one or two guards to search for firewood. This appeared to be the only job that the Japanese had ordered the Indians to keep us doing. It was exhausting and we heard from the men who had been out with the Indians that they were far worse than the Japanese because they beat the men and made them work harder.

We had had morning and evening roll call under the Japanese. Unless some silly ass had done something like getting caught buying something through the wire, it had been a fairly easy-going affair. The guards had just numbered us off and if the number of men tallied with his list we were dismissed quickly. Not so with the Indians. Now it was done with full military precision. Very few of us were in any condition to stand to attention while each of us had our names laboriously read out by some Indian.

After about ten days of Indian rule, word was passed around that we were leaving River Valley Camp and it was going to be taken over by the Indian Army. This was verified by our own officers. One day a new group of Japanese arrived to take us back to Changi. We started out before daybreak so as to be well on our way before the heat of the day. The Japs must have realized that a lot of us were in no fit state to walk fifteen miles and so had two trucks leap-frogging ahead of us to pick up any men who fell by the wayside. The trucks also carried food and water. Around midday the Japs stopped the march to feed us and gave us a welcome break for about two hours.

My own boots had long since fallen to pieces. It had become a custom at the camp that if anyone died their clothing was put into a pool to be distributed to other prisoners in need. Fortunately, for me I took a size 10½ in boots and at that time not too many men had feet that size. I was able to obtain a reasonably good pair. Also, I still had my sandals, which I regarded as my best wear. Strangely enough, even under the conditions we were in we had the urge to look as tidy as we could.

Eventually we arrived back at Changi. A lot of people think of Changi as the prison, but it is a whole village. I had spent about a year at the camp in River Valley.

Chapter 13

Changi

We were lucky to have volunteered our services to go to Singapore as tradesmen as I was told of some dreadful things that had happened in Changi while I was away. I will not detail them here as anything I know is only hearsay.

Again, I was not in Changi Prison but in some small building outside with seven other men from River Valley. Each week men were drafted out of Changi. They either went up country on the railway or down to Singapore to load the ships to take goods away to other places. This was sheer back-breaking work as it meant shifting hundred-weight bags of cement for hours on end, or 4gal cans of aviation spirit or petrol and many other heavy objects.

I was selected to go with a group on a trailer party. We got to where the firewood had been cut and the Japanese signalled that another man and I should stay on the trailer to stack it. I started to stack the timber and suddenly I got the urge to fart. The Jap was looking straight at me and, even to this day, I don't know what made me do it, but I pointed my fingers at him as though I had a gun and let go a real rip-roaring burst of fire. He looked at me for a moment and then screamed at me to get down off the trailer. As I was doing so, I thought, 'My God, I'm in for it now.' I was. He smacked my face a few times and gave me a couple of nasty body blows but, luckily, no rifle butt blows as sometimes happened. He then ordered me back up on the trailer. I think my dignity suffered more than my body.

I thought that was the end of the matter but later a couple of his mates turned up and they began smoking and talking. Then I saw him pointing at me and they were laughing amongst themselves; he had told them of the fart. He then came over and demonstrated that I should give a repeat performance for their benefit. By this time the pile of wood on the trailer had grown quite high and I had to perch on the top of it as best I could. Not only were the Japs watching but by this time the other prisoners had gathered around to watch my antics. Of course, farting was out of the question and so, taking aim, I blew the best raspberry of my life.

Chapter 14

Up Country

I had grown accustomed to life at Changi when our officers told us to be ready to move up country. In other words, we were bound for either Malaya or Thailand (or as it was then, Siam). This was the worst possible news for us as it meant that we were to be drafted to work on the dreaded railway line. I didn't know much about the line but one or two of the British or Aussies had somehow managed to get back to Changi from there and had brought back horrific stories of the so-called death camps. The Japanese had often used the threat of being sent to work on the railway line as a way of frightening us. I knew that even the Japs did not relish the idea of being sent to the railway.

One day we had to go to Singapore with our now meagre belongings. Quite a number of us had tried to find ways to miss being drafted, but it was no good. I was ill with what we called the 'shivers'. No-one knew what it was, but as soon as my temperature dropped even by a few degrees I started to shiver uncontrollably. All the strength left my body and all I could do was roll up in a blanket and wait for the shivering to stop. I suppose it was because we were under-nourished and also the local population had lots of diseases they were immune to, but we weren't. Anyway, the Japanese insisted that everyone was to leave the camp and so we made our pitiful way to Singapore. This time if any men collapsed the Japs just put them in trucks or wagons to continue the journey. The journey itself was a nightmare.

When we arrived in Singapore we were bundled onto waiting carriages. Once we were all on board the train started on its journey. All of this had an air of urgency about it – we were harassed by guards with shouts and, in some cases, blows from their rifles. If any of us had thoughts of escape, they were soon squashed when we saw that all the Japanese guards had fixed bayonets and the train had open trucks with manned machine guns mounted on them. We could see that these guards had been trained specifically to transport POWs.

We had been squashed into the carriages but somehow I had been fortunate enough to get a seat and once the journey started I collapsed unconscious. Many of the men were sick and needed to use the toilets on the train but this was almost impossible as the corridors were packed with men. The Japanese realized this and so the train was stopped at irregular intervals for men to relieve themselves. I tried to hang on as long as possible in case someone took my seat. Eventually the train stopped at a proper station and the Japs had food ready for us. We were not allowed to leave the train so the food was passed from one man to another. Even under these terrible conditions the prisoners shared. Each man was passed his fair share and, in some cases, you would see a man feeding his sick companion.

After I had had some food I began to feel a lot better and decided it was time I gave up my seat to someone else. Also, it had got unbearably hot in the compartment and I wanted some cooler air. Someone took my seat and I managed to squeeze my way to a window in the corridor. As the train chugged along all I could see was green jungle.

Eventually the train stopped at what appeared to be a fairly large shunting yard. Our train pulled in alongside another train which consisted of goods or cattle trucks. For some inexplicable reason we were ordered off the passenger train and on to the goods train and with the aid of the usual yelling and shouting and occasional blow or two from the Japs, we climbed aboard and packed ourselves in.

The journey in the carriages had been uncomfortable but this was far worse. Some of the trucks were wood and some were metal. I had more or less been pushed into a wooden cattle wagon which was reasonably clean so although I had to sit on the floor at least I wasn't sitting in dirt. Some of the other wagons were filthy.

The train trundled along at a slow pace and we had to sit with our backs against the side of the wagon. With the continuous jolting and bumping motions we were soon very sore. Fortunately, I was able to get up and move around now and again. The guards had not thought it necessary to lock us in so we were able to slide the door open and take turns at getting some fresh air. As we travelled through the jungle it was clear that this part of the line was quite new. The jungle had been recently cut back and the earth alongside the railway line had been turned over.

The train was now clanking and groaning more than ever. We had crossed a river a couple of times over wooden bridges that from a distance looked as though they were made of matchsticks. On one occasion the train had wound its way around a large bluff by means of a trestle bridge. A couple of the men were looking out of the door and told us to come. I looked out of the door and straight down into a river below. As the train wound round the bend we were able to see what we had crossed and it looked just like a shelf hanging on the edge of a cliff. This work had all been done by British and Australian prisoners.

We had been travelling for most of the day and evening was fast approaching when the train finally stopped. There was no sign of a station but an area had been cleared alongside the railway line. The area was occupied by a number of soldiers and some Thais who were preparing food in camp kitchens. We were told by an interpreter that we would be fed and that we would have to stay on the train overnight. In the morning we had to be prepared to walk to our destination.

Since leaving Singapore we had been travelling on the railway for two days and one night and had no idea where we were. Some men thought we were in Malaya, others in Thailand or even Burma. After I had been fed I slept as best I could but couldn't help wondering what morning would bring. Just after dawn we were roused by the Japanese yelling and shouting. We were given our small portion of rice and beans for breakfast. There had been no attempts at escape as the soldiers were well-armed and constantly patrolled up and down the train at night. Also, none of us had the skills to survive in the jungle on our own.

Whilst we were on the journey there had been no facilities for washing or for shaving. We were a sorry looking lot. Once again, we were gathered up into some semblance of order to move off on the march. We followed a well-defined track and before long found ourselves walking through a village. The occupants ignored us all as though this were a normal occurrence. Once through the village we found ourselves on a rough dirt road full of ruts and tracks which made it hard to walk. In the early afternoon the soldiers halted us and told us we were to rest for a few hours before starting on the march again.

Just before dusk we were lined up and fed. While we were eating, one of our officers told us that we were now going to spend all night marching to our destination. During the day we could rest. Someone asked him why we were to march only at night and the officer said he had no idea. All the Japanese told him was that night-time was better. I hardly had time to finish eating when we heard all kinds of strange noises around us. Lights began to appear and then a group of soldiers came towards us carrying hurricane lamps. The creaking noise was caused by three or four bullock carts loaded with the soldiers' gear.

Amidst the usual shouts and curses the guards soon had us on our merry way. The group that I was with was possibly between fifty to seventy-five men. Those up the front of the column at least had the benefit of light from the lamps. Those of us who were unfortunate enough to be in the rear could only stumble along as best we could.

The Japs seemed to have eyes like cats and could see in the dark. They walked alongside and to the rear of us and any straggling prisoners were urged on by shouts and curses. If that didn't make the stragglers keep up we heard the odd cry of pain as they received a blow from a fist or a rifle butt. These guards were totally different from any we had met before. Their job was to drive us like animals and they were accustomed to doing it.

I was not really aware of anything much as my whole concentration was just to put one foot in front of the other and keep going. At long last I began to notice a pale glow ahead of us. Somehow I had managed to keep up with the front runners and what I was seeing was the dawn breaking. In a short space of time there was enough daylight to see where I was walking and this made the going a lot easier. I was also able to be more observant of the area we were walking through. The track we were on was a rough dirt road full of ruts and hollows where the bullocks had travelled. Behind me I could hear the rumbling of the carts and looking back I saw that some of our men were slumped exhausted on the carts on top of the guards' gear. I couldn't help but wonder how long I would be able to keep going. Of course, I had no idea where we were going or how long the journey was going to last, so thinking about it was idle speculation.

After about an hour or so of daylight we came to a large clearing with a bamboo and palm leaf hut in it. The Japs stopped us and gave us to understand that we were to be fed and would rest there until evening. On this morning we were amazed to actually smell food cooking; it smelt like fish. It was a pleasant smell, not a fishy stink so we assumed that it was for the soldiers.

The order came for us to queue up for our food at a long bench outside the hut. The food was then brought out by some locals who started serving us. I had managed to hang on to my army mess tin which had two containers, a top and bottom half. A lot of the other men had only one bowl, some had only a mug. As I moved closer to the servery I could see there were two containers, one with rice and the other with some sort of stew. I held out my tin and was served a large ladle full of boiled rice. I then passed on to the next server who pointed to my empty tin to signal that I should hold that out as well and into this was poured a ladle full of soup. I sat on the ground with my back up against a tree and started my meal of salted fish soup and freshly boiled rice. When I had finished eating I felt satisfied for the first time in weeks. After I had eaten I made myself as comfortable as possible and went to sleep.

It seemed no time at all before we were awakened by the usual yells and shouts. We were fed again with a substantial vegetable soup. We realised they were feeding us better because they knew we couldn't carry on unless we had bigger rations. As we were eating our food an officer spoke to us in English, telling us that we must try and keep together on the march. There were bandits living in the jungle and they would rob, even kill, the stragglers. If we heard any shots being fired it was only the soldiers frightening off the bandits. We were sceptical about this and thought it was a ploy to make us keep together. We prepared to move off in the same way as the previous night, but with a different group of guards. As we left the camp I saw that several of our men were left behind, obviously too weak or sick to go on. I hate to think what happened to them.

When we started out this time I made sure that I was near the front. Having some light and, more importantly, a full stomach, made the night's journey a lot easier. Even so, it was still a nightmare just stumbling along and having the Japanese urging us on all the time. As one of them stopped talking another one started. As well, there was the continual creaking and groaning of the bullock carts. One day passed the same as another, as did the nights, and on and on we went into the jungle.

After living with the Japanese for so long I had become attuned to odd bits of conversation. One thing I kept hearing was, 'Chiang Mai'. This was often followed by some animated conversation and very often laughter and, in some cases, some suggestive gestures. It seemed to me that the guards were heading for Chiang Mai and that they expected to have a good time.

As far as I can remember, it was on the fifth day that we walked, or staggered, into what appeared to be a half-finished camp. Some huts had roofs but no walls, others walls but no roofs. This, we were told, was our destination. Our party was delegated to two huts with a roof on each. The guards told us that some locals would come later to finish the huts off. The huts followed the usual construction of a rough timber frame with the roof and walls covered with palm leaf thatch. On either side of a central gangway there was a raised bamboo platform about 60cm off the ground where we had to sleep. There was no ceremony about choosing a place to sleep; we just moved into the huts and flopped down in the first available space. Once we had settled ourselves down there was a total of ten men in my bay, including myself.

After I had rested for a while, two other men and I decided to explore the camp, not that there was much to see, just a collection of huts in various stages of construction. A short distance away from our huts we could see what appeared to be a more substantial building and we could see some soldiers moving to and fro. I could also hear the sound of a generator or motor. I was later to discover that it supplied lighting for them and also worked a water purifier. We also found out that the camp was built adjacent to a river. We were quite pleased about the river as we hoped it would enable us to bathe and wash what little clothing we had.

We met inmates and chatted about our journeys. One of the men had spent a period of time in Thailand and he estimated that we had walked about 180km through the jungle. He also thought that we were not too far from the Burmese border. A short time after we had met the other men, a couple of the Japanese must have seen us moving around. There were shouts and gestures making it quite clear that we were to go back to our huts.

Evening came and once again we were fed, but this time the ration was a lot smaller. As we queued for our food we were told that in the morning we would start working. I slept fitfully that night as I was feeling pangs of hunger and was worried about what awaited us in the morning. Dawn came and soon the Japs made us parade for our food, which was less than we had been given on the march. We still had not been given any opportunity to clean ourselves up so we looked and felt terrible. The British and Australian officers looked no different from us so it was obvious the Japs made no distinction between them and us, the other ranks.

As was the usual practice the Jap guard came and sorted us out into groups for working parties and as far as I could see no-one was excused, not even the really sick or lame men. The guards chose men at random and my party consisted of myself and five other men. None of us knew each other and our guard did not allow any of us to speak. We formed a line and were issued with shovels, picks, crowbars and other tools. I thought to myself, 'This is it, I'm going to die on this bloody railway.'

Several of the other parties had already moved off and in the distance we could hear the shouts of the Japanese and the clang of tools striking the ground. Our guard motioned for us to follow him and we moved off in a different direction from the other parties. I soon realized that we were going towards their living quarters. He stopped us some yards from the house and we were overwhelmed by a terrible stench – the latrine. It consisted of an open trench roofed over by thatch, and a long pole on which to sit.

Our guard, whom we called Jappy, split us up into two groups of three and through signs made us understand that one group was to fill in the old trench and the other group was to dig a new one. Unfortunately, I was chosen to dig the new trench. Admittedly the old one stunk to high heaven but at least it was easier to throw soil in than dig it out. Anyway, it didn't take too long to fill the latrine. Then Jappy went off, came back with a can of disinfectant and watered the ground with it. This made the work more bearable. We now had six men digging and we took it more or less upon ourselves to do a bit and rest a bit. As long as we kept going at a steady pace he seemed quite happy.

I judged it to be about midday when Jappy told us to 'Yasmay' (knock off) and signalled for us to follow him. He took us around the back of their house and motioned for us to wait for him. We waited a few minutes and he came back carrying a container made from half a 4gal petrol can. He put it down on the ground. It was filled with cold boiled rice with what looked like vegetables mixed into it.

Men from the Suffolk regiment surrendering to the Japanese in February 1942. This was the regiment in which Peter Jackson served. (Source: Wikipedia Commons)

Newspaper report of Peter's capture by the Japanese.

Lieutenant-General A.E. Percival signing the British surrender to Japanese in Singapore on 15 February 1942. Some 80,000 men were taken prisoner of war in Singapore and they joined the 50,000 already captured in Malaysia. (Source: D.O.W Hall, *Prisoners of Japan*, Historical Publications Branch, Wellington, 1948, reproduced with permission of the NZ Ministry for Culture and Heritage)

In Japanese Hands

Mrs. Margaret Jackson, of 80, Belmont-street, N.W.1, and formerly of Lady Margaret-road, N.W.5, whose husband, L/Sgt. Peter Richard Jackson, The Suffolk Regiment, was reported missing after the fall of Singapore, has just received notification that he is a prisoner in Japanese hands. L/Sgt. Jackson (portrait herewith) had been a member of the choir at St. Benet's Church, Lupton-street, N.W.5, since the age of six.

The Selarang Barracks crowded with 15,000 POWs. In August 1942, after some Australian POWs attempted to escape, the Japanese called on all the POWs to sign a 'No Escape Pledge'. Many of the POWs were crowded into the old British barracks designed to hold 1,200. Sanitation was almost non-existent. The POWs refused to sign for three days. On the third day the Japanese took the four Australians who had attempted to escape to Changi Beach and shot them in front of their commanding officers. At that stage the men voted to sign 'under duress'. (Source: D.O.W. Hall, *Prisoners of Japan*)

The cook house at the Selarang Barracks. (Source: D.O.W. Hall, *Prisoners of Japan*)

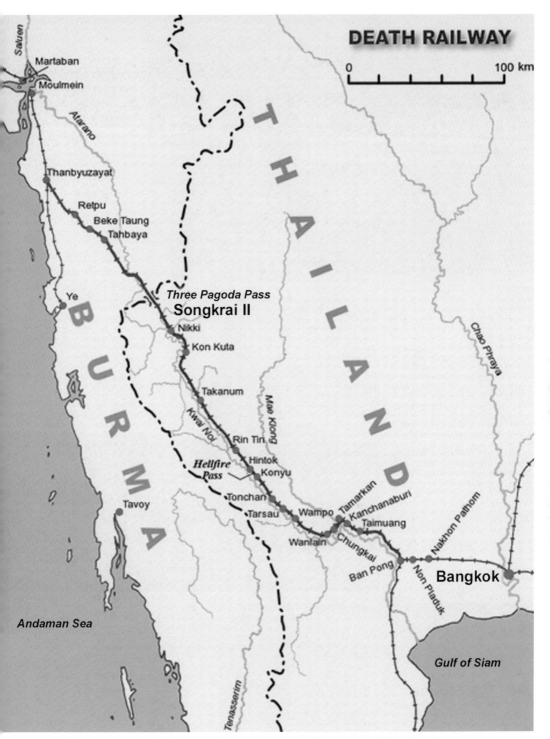

Map of the Thai-Burma Death Railway showing the probable position of Songkrai II.
(Source: Wikipedia Commons)

A well-established jungle camp. (Source: Thailand-Burma Railway Centre, Kanchanaburi)

Men in the Kanchanaburi Camp. The man on the left is wearing a 'Jap-happy', the loin cloth the men had to resort to when their clothes wore out. (Source: Thailand-Burma Railway Centre, Kanchanaburi, Thailand)

The interior of a typical accommodation hut. (Source: Thailand-Burma Railway Centre, Kanchanaburi, Thailand)

A train on the completed railway in 1944. (Source: Thailand-Burma Railway Centre, Kanchanaburi, Thailand)

The Wang Pho Viaduct. In 1943. It is one part of the railway that has survived and is now visited by people from all over the world who come to experience the railway and how it was built. It is maintained by the State Railway of Thailand. (Source Thailand-Burma Railway Centre, Kanchanaburi, Thailand)

A curved trestle bridge in the jungle. (Source Thailand-Burma Railway Centre, Kanchanaburi, Thailand)

A jungle trestle with a train crossing it. This was taken in 1943 when the railway was operational. It may be the Hintoku-Tampi railway bridge. This, like the one in the picture, was built of rough bush timber at a height of approximately 100 feet. A photograph of this bridge taken in October 1945 showed that it survived Allied bombing. (Source Thailand-Burma Railway Centre, Kanchanaburi, Thailand)

The railway track from Kanachanaburi photographed in October 1945. (Source: D.O.W. Hall, *Prisoners of Japan*)

The ceremony held to mark the opening of
the railway at Konkoita on 25 October 1943.
The railway on which work started in May
1942 was completed in seventeen months.
(Source: Thailand-Burma Railway Centre,
Kanchanaburi, Thailand)

Prisoners of War building a railway bridge.
The artist, Murray Griffin, hid this sepia
drawing between sheets of tin stopping the
leaks in the attap roof of his hut. Griffin was
captured by the Japanese after the fall of
Singapore and sent to Changi. He survived
and returned to Australia in 1945. (Source:
D.O.W. Hall, *Prisoners of Japan*)

A jungle chapel built by the prisoners and
drawn from memory by Peter Jackson.

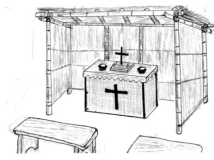

The cholera hospital at Hintok. This was painted by Jack Chalker whose studies as an Art student were interrupted by the Second World War. He was captured in Singapore and endangered his life by sketching the inhumane conditions in the camps. The drawings were hidden in sections of bamboo, buried in the ground, hidden in the attap roofs of huts and even placed in artificial legs used by the amputees. (Source: D.O.W. Hall, *Prisoners of Japan*)

(*Left*) Peter at forty, sometime after he arrived in New Zealand. (*Right*) Peter's mother taken not long before she died. She is aged eighty-eight.

He chattered away in Japanese and I caught the words *mishi* (rice or food) and *taxan* (a lot) and *yasmay* (stop work). I gathered from his signs that the food he had brought out to us was leftovers and was a reward for working hard. We pointed out that we had no plates or utensils to eat with. His answer to that was quite simple; he just put his hand into the tin and scooped out a handful and ate it from his hand. After wiping his hand he pointed on the ground and drew a half-circle in the dirt with a line down the centre, which we took to mean half-an-hour. With that he disappeared back into the hut. The other men and I said to hell with hygiene and were soon scooping out the food from the tin. It tasted all the better because this was an unexpected bonus.

True to his sign language, Jappy appeared again in about half-an-hour and took us back to our job. We kept working steadily the rest of the day and must have made a satisfactory job of the trench as he indicated that the next day our job would be to shift the wooden superstructure and place it over the trench we had just dug. We went back to camp once more and queued up for our meal – again, it was small.

I spoke to the other men who were my neighbours in the hut and they told me they had spent the day working on the railway. They were absolutely exhausted as it entailed a lot of heavy lifting and the Japanese kept bullying them. They also told me they had had no midday break and the only thing the Japs had given them were drinks of water. I told them what I and my gang had been doing but didn't dare mention the food. That would have been very cruel and also the whole camp would have tried to take the job my party was doing.

The next morning Jappy came to collect us. We gathered our tools and hey-hoed off to work. We did the job of shifting the shelter quite satisfactorily. Unfortunately, there was no food. Instead he brought out a bucket of tea for us to share. Later he shared out a packet of English cigarettes.

On the third day our guard took us to a hut a little further away and showed us a large heap of gravel, the same type that they put down under railway tracks. We didn't need to guess where it had come from. There were several paths round their quarters leading to latrines and other outbuildings, also a long one leading to our camp, which we used daily. These tracks were very rough and Jappy demonstrated that we were to level them and spread the shingle to make a better path. This was obviously going to be hard work but I was sure it was better than working on the railway where our friends had told us that the Japs were constantly harassing the workers and that a lot of the men were on the verge of collapsing.

We set to work and, as I said before, as long as we worked steadily Jappy seemed quite content. We called our guard Jappy because he never told us his name. He spoke no English, but I could pick out a few Japanese words which sometimes helped us to understand what he wanted. He did not like us talking to each other and so, other than the odd word here and there, we spent most of the day in silence. We carried on working with him for about five days doing the paths. It was a time-consuming job and he always gave us a break at midday and let us have some small item of food or a drink, or a cigarette. We were allowed to go to the river and wash ourselves and our clothing, which meant we could keep ourselves clean to some extent.

In the early hours of the sixth day we awoke to hear one of the men in our bay being violently ill. We just took it that he had eaten something that had disagreed with his stomach. A lot of the men had tried all sorts of berries and plants from the jungle with disastrous results. When morning came we realized that he was really ill and needed attention. The soldiers had allowed us to have a sick bay with a medical orderly, and so one of us went to report that our friend was very ill. Two men came and took him away on a stretcher.

That same morning Jappy came to take us to work and we thought he didn't seem his usual self. We started working on the paths and it became clear that Jappy was also ill. He kept disappearing into the scrub and we could hear him being sick. Later, he became worse and he was frequently in the latrine. We couldn't help but feel sorry for him, enemy though he was, and so we just kept on working as though nothing was wrong. Eventually he signalled to us to stop work and through sign language told us to go back to the camp on our own, which of course, we were glad to do.

I expected a new guard to come for us the next day to replace Jappy, but no-one turned up. This worried me as I thought it meant we would have to work on the railway. We talked it over and agreed that it would be best to carry on working on the paths as we were obviously meant to complete the job. We worked through the day and queued up for our food with the rest of the men. The next morning we had our breakfast, a small portion of rice and boiled beans with a little salt added, and were preparing to get our tools when one of our officers came and spoke to us about the job we were doing. One of the Japs in charge of the camp had told him that Jappy was very ill and that there were no other guards to replace him. As we were working in close proximity to their quarters we could carry on with what we were doing as it was important to get the paths done before the rainy season set in. The Japs must have been keeping an eye on us as a fresh pile of shingle had appeared overnight.

Of the ten men in my bay of the hut, my two friends and I seemed to be holding our own health-wise, but we were undernourished. Two men had gone into the Sick Bay seriously ill and others looked due to go at any time. The Japs were very tough and unless you were at death's door you were forced to work. After about ten days in camp many of the men were really ill with vomiting and dysentery. It wasn't only the prisoners who were getting sick but some of the Japanese as well. Finally, we realized that the camp was suffering a cholera epidemic.

As far as we prisoners were concerned, survival would depend entirely on the man's constitution. There was no medication for us. I suspect that the Japanese fared little better. The few British and Australian officers who had come with us were no better off than were the rest of us. Admittedly they did not have to work as hard as the men; their main function appeared to be to issue orders on behalf of the Japs. As far as food and clothing was concerned, they had the same as us. In a very short space of time there were only three of us left in our bay of the hut: Joe, Taffy and me.

That night Joe and Taffy told me that they had made friends with a sergeant who was coming to visit us to talk about something very important. Morning came and Ian arrived. Before he started to tell us why he had come he swore us to complete secrecy. He said it was a matter of life and death. Things were bad in the camp. Men were being beaten up for having a piddle without asking permission. Even a look of disapproval or a muttered word was dangerous as the Japs were always in a filthy mood.

Ian started by telling us that he had been fortunate, or unfortunate, enough to have been shifted upcountry with his platoon officer and that they had been able to maintain a friendly relationship. Although the officers were segregated from the other ranks, as we were called, we were still able to visit them if we wished. Ian had

91

been to visit his friend and found him very ill. Within a matter of hours his friend had died but he had entrusted his few meagre belongings to Ian. On looking through his friend's pack Ian had found a few items of clothing and some personal letters from his family giving his address Also in the pack was a rolled up towel which contained a rolled up page of an atlas and an army compass, and also a broken watch. Had the Japanese found these things hidden in the officer's belongings I am sure he would have been beaten up, or even killed, for they were prohibited for British or Australian prisoners.

Ian's brother, Bernard, who was a corporal, was also in the camp. They had decided that it was prudent to keep the compass, watch and map a secret. Early one morning, when all was quiet, they had spent some time orienting the map and compass to find out where we were. The river we were near was of medium size and quite fast flowing which seemed to denote it had come some distance before reaching our camp. Orienting the compass due north showed that the river flowed south which meant, hopefully, that it was flowing towards the Gulf of Siam.

Ian and Bernard had also heard the Japs mentioning Chiang Mai. From these clues they had deduced that we were possibly on the Me Ping River or, if not, at least a tributary flowing into it. This meant that if someone went against the current up the river they could eventually reach Burma or China.

The two brothers had also met a man named Eddie who in civilian life had been a civil engineer. He had worked in Thailand, Malaya and Indonesia. He spoke the local languages as well as a small amount of Japanese. Eddie had been a volunteer Singapore soldier and was captured in uniform. The other person whom they named was a private soldier named Fred; he had been batman to the deceased officer and knew something of his personal life. Ian, Bernard, Eddie and Fred had decided they had no wish to stay in the camp to die either of starvation, of overwork on the railway, or of cholera. A slight complication had arisen when a man named Jimmy was transferred to Ian and Bernard's hut and overheard some of their conversation. He was a sergeant and on that basis they decided to include him if he wished. With regard to Joe and Taffy, they had known Ian in Singapore and as they seemed reasonably fit it was decided they too could join the group.

I was wondering why I was being brought into this crazy gang. This was simple: food. Taffy and Joe had known that my work around the Japanese quarters had given me a good knowledge of the camp layout. I had also been involved in making a path to a store where the food was kept. I had remarked that considering our meagre rations, there was enough loose rice lying around the store to feed an army. We had naturally assumed that it would be guarded day and night but I had noticed that the door had no bolt or padlock on it and swung to and fro with the wind.

It appeared that Eddie had overheard some Japs talking. They had said that many of their men were sick and they had only enough men to supervise the working parties. Another time he had heard that our Japanese soldiers were hoping to be relieved in the near future. We knew the only hope we had of getting away from the camp depended on getting supplies of food. We held a council of war and I was included in the group. We were all quite aware that our lives hung in the balance whatever we did.

It was decided that I should lead the way to the food store to test whether it was guarded. I warned whoever was going that whatever they did they must not tread on the gravel as it would crunch horrendously and would warn anyone around. Bernard and Taffy volunteered to go with me that night to see how things went. We each armed ourselves with a scoop. I had a mug, Bernard also had a mug, and Taffy a tin. We were going to use the dead officer's pack to carry whatever we found.

Taffy and I lay on our beds waiting until the whole camp was quiet. I dozed off but Taffy shook me and said he thought it was moonlight enough to see where we were going. I agreed and so we went to the next hut for Bernard who was awake and waiting for us. There were rarely clear skies overhead, but the moon did give quite a good light. We set off barefoot on our mission. My heart was beating like a hammer. It seemed so loud, I was sure someone would hear it. Fortunately, the ground we walked on had been trodden flat so it was not hard on our bare feet. Even so, each step was agony as we tried not to make any noise. When we reached the shingle track that led to the storehouse I made sure that we kept on the soft ground at the side of the path. This proved more difficult walking as there were a lot of loose twigs and dirt around. Slowly, ever so slowly, hardly daring to breathe, we crept up to the hut.

Finally, I got to the door and it swung loosely on its hinges. We stood motionless. There was not a sound, just dead silence.

We had made no plan of action but it just seemed natural that, as Taffy had the bag and I had tried the door, we both went in. Taffy held the bag and started to fill it. There seemed to be rice everywhere – sacks of it – I was actually kneeling in it. Meanwhile, Bernard was standing guard outside. Of course, I couldn't see what I was doing, I could only feel the cup filling, and the noise of rice going into the cup and the bag seemed deafening in the silence. After a few minutes I felt Taffy's hand on mine to stop filling the pack and he whispered, 'Getting heavy.' With that I gathered up one or two handfuls of rice and scattered them around hoping to cover up the mug marks in the heap. We got back to the hut without incident and parted company with Bernard. Back in the hut I was so exhausted I went to sleep almost straight away.

I awoke in the morning with a real fright as I could hear a Jap yelling and shouting outside our hut. At first I thought he had come for me or Taffy, but he was shouting at some poor devil who was too sick to even stand up. I got my breakfast and of the original six men I was working with there were now only four. Two were either sick or dead, we didn't know as we were discouraged from going anywhere near the Sick Bay. In any case, the stench was enough to keep us away.

We drew our usual shovels, rakes and wheelbarrow and went off to our job. I thanked God the Japanese had a path mania for it seemed we had no sooner finished one than they needed another one. The Japs had now given us instructions that if they wanted a path made we would see some sticks with white cloth tied on them and that denoted where it would start and finish. This morning there was a whole row of sticks and flags leading from the main path to the long-drops. 'Great,' I thought, 'this will keep us busy for a while.' We started levelling the ground and all the time I was watching out to see if there were any Japs around. I expected at any minute they would want to use the lavatories. I could hear the sound of men working in the distance and the Japs voices, but they didn't seem to be as noisy as they used to be. At that moment I had a crazy idea and taking a rake went along the main path and branched off to where the rice store was. The path looked quite rough and so I busied myself raking and levelling it to look tidy. I deliberately made as much noise as I could, thinking that if there were any Japs around this should bring them running, but there was not one in sight.

I took my courage in my hands and pushed open the door of the store and looked inside. At a quick glance I could see about eight to ten bags of rice as well as the open ones that had spilt out onto the floor. On a shelf on the left were some wooden boxes and the top one was open. I put my hand into it and felt something that almost felt like leather strips. I pulled it out and realised immediately that it was a piece of salted and dried fish. Boiled in water it makes quite a decent tasting fish soup. What a discovery! I got out of that store like a rabbit out of a hole, in case someone saw me. I went back to the gang and carried on with our job, but was quite cheered by my find and couldn't wait to tell Joe and Taffy.

Once the other members of the party knew of the dried fish, it was decided that we should take it in turns to visit the storehouse, two at a time; one to keep a lookout and one to take the food. Taffy, Bernard and I had already taken our turn so it was left to the others to have a go. After the second night, when Ian and Fred had gone to the store, it was clear that the hut was not guarded. I dared not go near the store again in the day as I had no idea at all what the Japs did about rationing, whether it was a daily routine or just a haphazard visit when they needed something.

It did not take long to fill the pack with rice, but it was too heavy for one man to carry by himself. We estimated it weighed about 30lbs. Also, it was a very difficult thing to hide, so we decided to split it up into smaller lots. Fortunately, all of us had some sort of bag. After some time, we held another council of war and decided that enough food had been collected. To take any more was too dangerous. By now we had all agreed that an escape bid was a real possibility.

Men were becoming sick at an ever increasing rate, and more and more were actually dying of cholera. Both the men that I was working with and the escape party were dreadfully afraid that they would catch the terrible disease. I was worried about it myself.

I could not understand the mentality of the Japanese. While we were marching to the camp our food had been increased, apparently to get us to the railhead. It was quite obvious that they wanted the railway pushed on as quickly as possible. Why they were feeding us at starvation level now, I couldn't understand, especially when I had seen rice that was literally going to waste. Also, as men were dying, there were even fewer to feed. My only suggestion is that there were so few Japanese guards (and they were getting fewer daily), that they were afraid that if we were kept fit and well we prisoners may have revolted and tried to attack them. That, or they were just sheer bloody-minded and enjoyed making us suffer.

We decided that we should make our escape attempt on Sunday morning, 6 June 1943, at dawn. We had already done a couple of dummy runs by pretending to go to the lavatory very early in the morning. It was quite clear that there was no-one about at that time. We arranged to assemble at the back of one of the huts furthest away from the Japanese quarters. After a fitful night's sleep, we gathered there in semi-darkness and set off into the jungle. The jungle was mainly bamboo, and not thick scrubby growth, so we were able to move with relative ease. It became even easier when daybreak came.

We were just congratulating ourselves that we had got away when we came to a steep bank above the river. We had more or less come to a dead end, or so we thought, until someone said that there was a path or track on the far side. The river at that point was about 30ft wide and fairly fast flowing. We had no idea of the depth but we knew we had to cross it to get away. Otherwise we would have to abandon the attempt or try another track. Although none of us relished the idea, we opted to cross the river. We decided that we would try to form a human chain by holding each other's hands and so one by one we stepped into the cold water. Fortunately, it seemed the water, although fast flowing, was no more than waist deep.

We were busily helping each other across when suddenly the silence was shattered by the sound of someone starting up a motor quite near us. After a few abortive attempts, it broke into a full throated roar like the sound of a motorbike engine. It was the generator starting up for the day to work the Jap's water purifier and give them electricity. It sounded so close that it almost caused us to panic but so far we were still hidden from view.

We crossed the river safely and once on the track on the other side we looked down river but couldn't see anything, so the noise must have been further away than we had thought. All of us breathed sighs of relief. We were aware of the dangers, but at least we had taken our destiny into our own hands.

Chapter 15

The Great Escape

Across the river we found a well-defined track that was used by the locals. We oriented our compass and assumed that the river flowed from north to south. This could only be a guess as the river could possibly have taken a U-turn at some point and been flowing in the opposite direction.

We decided to keep going as long as possible, to put as much distance as we could between us and the Japs. We took compass bearings at different points along the river and each time we appeared to be going north. The track was difficult. As soon as we'd gone a few hundred yards we had to cross the river. This was exhausting as the river was fast-flowing and we had difficulty keeping our feet. We were in danger of being swept away. We were continually wet but it was a waste of time drying ourselves as we never knew when we would round another bend to find another river crossing. Finally, we decided that we would have to stop as we were tired and hungry, having started the day on an empty stomach. We found a place where we could move off the main track and, taking care not to disturb the jungle, worked our way in to a small clearing where we hoped to escape notice if any locals passed by.

During the time that we had been preparing the escape Eddie had contacted some Thais. He spoke the language and was able to buy or barter for a few necessities, the most important being a few boxes of matches. He drew one out and within a short space of time we had a small bamboo fire going. We decided to cook some rice and dried fish, which was slow as the only cooking utensil we had was my mess tin. We had wanted to fill our water bottles but we could use only river water. The Japs were the only ones with access to purified water, although even that was suspect. But both the rice and fish had to be boiled in river water, although we all suspected that it was this that carried the cholera bugs. I cooked some rice and some fish and shared it out equally among the eight of us, and then cooked another lot so that we satisfied our hunger.

Once we had eaten, we had a council of war. Eddie was all for pushing on again. The rest of us pointed out that we had found a good spot to camp and that we may have to go a long way before we found anywhere as good. It was dark so I just rolled myself in my blanket and went to sleep.

We woke early the next morning and decided that rather than take time to cook any food we would just boil some drinking water. We had found the previous day that we suffered from thirst as much as from hunger. As soon as we got on the track we were crossing the river again and again. At times we looked across the river and were sure we had done a u-turn, as we thought it was the same rocky bank we had passed a quarter-of-an-hour previously. We had no way of telling the time.

Further up the river the track deteriorated – it was very muddy and badly eroded at some of the river crossings and we had a hard time getting a foothold. When we came to a particularly bad patch of track we found large footprints. Eddie told us that they were elephant tracks and it was obviously a village track. We were to keep a sharp lookout for Thai travellers.

Day followed day and several times we saw other tracks that joined the one we were following. Eddie had no doubt that these tracks led to villages. We were always on the alert so that if we met up with anyone we could quickly get off the track. We took it in turns to lead the way along the track and agreed that at any sign of danger we would get off as soon as possible. Then it happened. Our leader stopped suddenly, raised his hand and waved us urgently off the track. We hid ourselves quickly and soon we could hear people talking to one another. As the voices came nearer I heard a strange swishing sound and the ground was vibrating. I peeped through the bamboo in time to see a large grey shape passing. It was an elephant with a small party of locals going the other way. This was the first time that we had seen any sign of life since we had left the railway camp. It cheered us up because we knew the track must lead somewhere.

Not too long after the elephant passed we rounded a bend and the jungle thinned out. As we got further along the track we could see the outline of roofs. At this point Eddie took command. He told us to hide while he went forward to spy out the land. He hoped he would be able to talk to any villagers he met. He disappeared and we waited in nervous anticipation for his return about ten or fifteen minutes later. He told us he had been around the village and it appeared to be deserted. There were fresh graves and he thought people had recently been buried. He suggested we leave one man guarding the track entering the village and one at the other end leaving the village. They would warn us if anyone was coming.

We explored the village and soon found that what he said was true. The huts were of bamboo and palm leaves, and raised about 6ft off the ground with an open space beneath. Each hut had a bamboo ladder leading up to the doorway. There were eight of these living huts and a larger one which looked to me like a communal meeting house. Eddie told us that visitors slept in the head man's hut. In the centre of this hut was a stone slab which had been used as a fireplace. We could see that a fire had burnt there recently. Many of the trees had been badly damaged and there were loose leaves and twigs everywhere; also a couple of piles of elephant dung. Eddie thought the party that had passed us earlier had either camped overnight or stopped for a meal.

We decided that we would take a chance and explore the rest of the huts and so each of us chose one to explore. Mine was quite clean except for a thin layer of dust from disuse. On the floor was a rush matting which I thought might be handy but when I tried to roll it up it felt stiff and heavy so I decided to leave it where it was. There was a shelf made of bamboo slats and on it were some clay pots which looked well-used, but none had lids or tops. The first one I looked into had some evil smelling fatty stuff. The next had some whitish looking crystals in it. Hesitantly, I wet my finger and dipped it in the crystals, touching my tongue I found that it was salt. Two other jars held mouldy looking leaves, probably some sort of herbs.

Find number two was a black iron cooking pot with a bucket handle. It looked to me to be just about the right size for our party to cook in. I then noticed some bamboo pots hanging from the roof. One had a lid on it and as soon as I took the lid off knew that it contained tobacco. Jackpot! I decided to leave things as they were and see how the other boys had fared. It seemed that each of us had found something useful. There was one hut we had not searched but as soon as I got near it I stopped dead, I knew the smell immediately – cholera – so we gave that one a very wide berth.

We decided not to stay in the village and retreated back into the jungle alongside the track. We could see that the huts in the village had not been disturbed, except by us, and decided that the next morning we would take anything useful that we could carry.

Eddie went to get Fred who was guarding the far end of the track and both came back carrying two large handfuls of bananas – it was an exciting find. Eddie, bless him, had spotted a banana plant. We got a fire going and instead of dried fish we had rice and bananas.

The next morning Eddie suggested that it would be better to go to the village early, get what we could and move on as soon as possible. He was emerging as our leader. Eddie visited each hut with whoever had explored it and chose what we should take. Weight was the most important consideration as we had to carry everything on our backs. I showed Eddie my finds and he chose the salt and the cooking pot; the tobacco got an emphatic, 'No'. It could be smelt metres away and if anyone passed nearby it would guide them to us. He warned me not to mention it to the others as he didn't want to start any arguments.

Taffy and Joe overcame their repugnance at the last minute and decided to visit what we called the 'cholera hut'. It was just as well because when they came out Taffy was holding a small sack which, on inspection, proved to hold about 2 or 3kg of edible dried beans. As they had to be cooked by boiling, they were safe to eat.

We tallied up our finds. We had four small light sleeping mats, salt, dried beans, some fresh chilli peppers and bananas and, at last, a decent cooking pot. We had not been lucky enough to find any rice but Eddie said the beans would be a good substitute. After sharing out our loads we were on our way.

Soon we were climbing up a gradient. Although the river had narrowed it was now running much faster and it was beginning to be much more difficult to keep on our feet when we crossed from one side to the other. After leaving the deserted village we met two other elephant parties. Luckily, each time, we spotted them in time to hide. We were quite sure that this was a regular elephant trail and that sooner or later we would either meet someone or come to a village.

By now our rice stock was nearly exhausted. The beans had a strange musty smell even after we had boiled them for a long time in salted water. So far the weather had been kind to us, except for some drizzle, so we were able to sleep in the open each night.

The track twisted and turned so much that we could rarely see more than a few metres ahead. On this particular day we heard the sound of river water rushing along but couldn't see where the noise was coming from. I was in the lead and as I turned a sharp bend I saw a torrent of water surging down between two large rocky outcrops. I waited for the others to catch up and we studied it for a while, wondering how we would negotiate this barrier. Eventually, we found the elephant track running into the jungle and after a steep climb we got to the top of the waterfall. There the countryside opened out onto a plateau and the river had formed a small lake which looked clear and clean. I was tempted to drink some as we were all sick and tired of drinking boiled water.

On looking around this area we could see it was well-used as a camp site. A ring of stones had been set up to form a fireplace and the elephants had been tethered near the trees so that they could feed themselves. We were all in agreement that this was no place for us and hurried on. We were soon out of the clearing and on a jungle path. Frequently we lost sight of the river but the sound was quite loud. Finally, I realized that we were climbing a hill with the river well below us in a ravine.

After walking for some time we came to a fork in the track. One track continued straight ahead and probably followed the river, and the other branched off to the right. It was more used than the straight ahead track. Once again, we looked to Eddie for advice. He believed that the right-hand track led to a village, where there were likely to be Japs. We decided to go straight ahead.

All of us now tired easily as we were malnourished. We found the uphill-going exhausting. Finally, we came to a small patch of level ground where the river took a sharp turn. Above the clear space was a large rocky bluff whose overhang was like a roof. We agreed that this was an ideal place to spend the night and to hell with the chance of being caught. There were signs that other people had camped there before, even a pile of dry sticks left for somebody to start a fire with. Eddie was nervous and was not too happy about stopping as he thought that someone may return here to camp. However, we soon had a fire going and decided that we should empty our food bags and have one last meal and let the future look after itself. We finished the rice, beans and dried fish stew and went to sleep.

Some time during the night I awoke to the sound of heavy rain. It was teeming down but, other than a few splashes on my face, I kept

101

dry. In the morning I was awoken by loud voices and for a moment thought that someone had found us. It was our men excitedly pointing out that the river had risen overnight and was about an inch away from my feet, and still rising. I was up in a flash, gathering up my sparse belongings in seconds.

The overnight rain did not make things any easier for us. The track was muddy and we slipped and slid all over the place. We were feeling depressed and I thought that I didn't care if the Japs caught me. Anything was better than what we were going through. We had not been walking very long when we came to another fork in the track. Again, one seemed to follow the river, the other branched to the right. The right-hand track looked as though it had not been used for a while and so we decided it might lead somewhere where we could rest unobserved.

After a short time we could see the outline of thatched roofs, and knew we were coming to a village. We got as near as we dared and Eddie once again volunteered to go forward to spy out the land. He came back saying it was probably another deserted village. This time we just walked straight in, not even bothering to post sentries. We found a dry spot under one of the huts where we plonked ourselves down for a rest.

Eventually we pulled ourselves together and started exploring. I could hear running water and found a small clear stream running down a rocky gully. I called to the others. We still had a reasonable supply of tea, so decided we would have a brew-up of 'chai'. It took no time at all to get a small fire going and Eddie told us he had just used the last match of a box of fifty. He had taken over the job of lighting the fires and seemed quite expert at it. By his reckoning he had used an average of two matches per day, so we had been on the track for approximately twenty-five days.

As we drank the tea we studied our surroundings. This village looked larger than the previous one. It looked older and more permanent. We started to think about where to spend the night and unanimously decided to stay right where we were. The stream I had found came down through a small rocky gully so it appeared safe to drink.

Our next thought was food. We decided to have a look around the *kampong* (village) to see if we could find anything. The *kampong* followed the same layout as the previous one, but with a larger meeting hut in the centre of the living quarters. Eddie thought it would be quicker to explore the place in pairs. So, Bernard and Ian, Taffy and Joe, and Jimmy and Fred went off to search the huts, while Eddie and I went to see if there were any fruit trees around. We found a track at the back of the meeting hut and not far away was a patch of ground that had been cultivated. My knowledge of gardening was nil, so what Eddie was looking for was a mystery to me.

We found a patch of green leaves and, using a large penknife he carried, Eddie started to dig. In a few moments he'd pulled out a reddish looking object. He asked me if I knew what it was and I said I thought it looked like a potato. I was nearly right: it was a sweet potato and delicious when cooked. Eddie soon had a pile of about a dozen. He thought that was enough for a meal. As the potatoes were quite large Eddie suggested we boil some and bake others in the fire. I washed them in the stream and filled the cooking pot with fresh water. The others had built up a nice big fire and very soon we were having a banquet.

As we ate we talked of what we had discovered in the huts. As it was nearly dark we decided to leave any further explorations until the next day. We retired to sleep in the big meeting house, which was quite fortunate as it rained very heavily in the night.

The nights were getting colder and we'd found that if two or even three men slept close together we had the use of three blankets instead of one. So, all bunched up, we slept well. Thankfully, the morning dawned bright and cheerful and we were soon moving around. We had nothing for breakfast so just decided to continue to look through the huts. There appeared to be no reason why the village was deserted, for it was tidy and the huts in reasonable repair. Eddie's theory was that the Japs had rounded up the villagers and taken them to use as slave labour. They may have been clearing the jungle for the railway camps.

Our discoveries were a *parang* (a large heavy knife used for chopping or hacking), a ball of heavy twine and a tinder box. This last item proved to be of great value. It was a small bamboo box containing a piece of stone and a piece of steel sitting in what looked like a bed of dried grass. Again, it was Eddie who showed us how to use it. You take out a small quantity of the dried tinder (grass or bark), then you strike the stone (flint) with the steel, which makes a spark. These fall on to the tinder, which you then blow on, with the result that there is a small blaze to light a larger dry piece of wood.

We also found a bag containing some rice that smelt a little musty but appeared edible when washed, a bamboo container of salt and, best of all, half a box of salted dried fish. At least our immediate food problem was solved.

Suddenly, we heard a thumping noise coming from behind one of the huts. It was a regular bomp, bomp, bomp and, on peeping cautiously round the corner, we saw Eddie working some contraption with his foot. Set in the ground was a hollowed out log about the size of a bucket. Further away were two stakes driven into the ground and mounted on these was a long arm. On the end of the arm was another piece of wood, making what looked like a large hammer. The hammerhead thumped into the hollowed out bucket-like log. The other end of the arm, or bar, was pushed down by the foot which raised the hammerhead and let it drop into the bucket. This contraption was used to de-husk rice; we called it a paddy pounder. A few handfuls of rice were placed into the bucket and pounded until it had been de-husked. This was then taken out of the bucket and winnowed in the old-fashioned way, by throwing it up in the air. The wind blows the husks away and leaves the rice in the winnowing tray.

Nearby was a small shed which contained some small wooden bins of unhusked rice. This prompted us to try out the paddy pounder and we found that it worked. We had no trouble finding a winnowing tray and, although far from being experts, we were soon producing quite reasonable looking rice.

Eddie said that he had been thinking about the rotted goods we had found and he was sure they were either fruit or vegetables. We found a small banana plantation but most of the trees had been badly damaged. It looked as though they had been slashed deliberately and the crop destroyed. There were, however, other fruit trees. We found a large jackfruit (breadfruit), some mangoes, paw-paw and durian. Durian have a very bad smell, like fresh horse manure, but if you can cope with the smell long enough to scrape out the fruit, it has a thick custard-like texture and a pleasant taste. Although the vegetable patch was very overgrown, there were rows of green stuff that looked like spinach and a root vegetable similar to a parsnip. I have no doubt that had we known more about the jungle we could have lived far better than we did.

By the time we had finished exploring it must have been about noon, so we built up the fire and prepared a meal. The root vegetables tasted similar to a turnip or swede and as we suffered no ill-effects we pronounced them edible. There were no signs of cholera having affected the village, so it was great to be able to use the fresh water from the stream for both drinking and washing.

We decided to spend the rest of the day sorting out our few possessions. I had managed to retain a spare pair of shorts and a shirt. My boots were quite badly worn but I still had the sandals I had found in Singapore. I had tried to conserve my footwear by going barefoot whenever the track was easy and, as it was well-used, at times I could go quite long distances without too much discomfort.

We would have loved to stay in the village but we knew we could be discovered at any time. Someone said they were curious about the stream as it seemed to be going in the wrong direction to link up with the river we were following. Ian and Bernard volunteered to take the compass to see if they could follow it and see where it was going.

Eddie thought there was a larger village along the track we had turned off earlier on. He was worried about the possibility of Japs. We all agreed that to stay in the village was too dangerous. We had to push on up river.

After about an hour or so Bernard and Ian came back and said that as far as they could tell the stream went in a different direction altogether to our river. They had also found another quite well-used track that crossed the stream not too far away from where we were.

We decided that early the next day we would move on. We spent the rest of that day gathering as much rice and other food as we were able to carry. As we were about to leave, Jimmy reminded us to fill our water bottles from the stream. He also thought it would be a good idea to destroy any evidence that we had visited the village.

We got back to the track and followed the river, going uphill. The track was becoming more rocky and the river was becoming more turbulent. Fortunately, we only had one crossing to make that day and found clear calm water. We saw elephant tracks and droppings, but Eddie thought they were fairly old and the track had not been used for some time.

Chapter 16

The Friendly Villages

We had been on the track for some days and had lost all sense of time. Once again, our food stocks were sadly depleted and now it rained constantly. We were wet most of the time. The jungle had changed from mainly bamboo to larger trees and often the track was blocked by undergrowth and we had to hack our way through it.

One day we came to a side track and decided to explore it. After walking for some time, someone whispered, 'Huts ahead'. We had stopped to appraise the situation when we heard the unmistakable noise of a bleating goat. We soon discovered three huts opening out on to a clearing at the end of the track. On the far side of the clearing, looking at us very nervously, was a goat with three kids. We couldn't believe our luck; real live meat sent from Heaven. We thought we would explore the huts first. They looked as though they had been deserted for some time. There was nothing of value to us. We fanned out to approach the goats, but they seemed to know what we were planning and took off into the scrub. After about half an hour of chasing them around, we caught one. It put up a hell of a struggle and bleated in a pitiful manner. As we walked away we could hear the nanny crying out. We passed the kid from one to another and gradually it seemed to calm down. The question arose: how do we kill it? Cut its throat? Can't do that, knife's too blunt. Break its neck? Can't, not strong enough. Hit it on the head with a rock? No volunteers. Put its head in the fork of a tree and two of us break its neck? Again, no volunteers. I remember having tears in my eyes and saying something like, 'We can't kill the poor little bugger. I am going to take it back to its mother.' No-one disagreed, so I carried it back along the track and delivered it safely to its mother. Their reunion was a joy to watch. When I got back to the others not a word was said. But there was no goat stew.

A day or so after the goat incident, we suddenly found the track came out into an open space and, without realizing it, we had come upon an occupied village. We dodged back hoping we hadn't been spotted. It was quiet, although we had seen people moving about.

After a short discussion we decided Eddie would go into the village. Even if we had to give ourselves up it was better than enduring more hardship. We could not see what was happening, but there seemed to be quite a commotion and we all thought Eddie had been captured. That made us very nervous. Eddie seemed to have been gone a long time. Then we heard him calling, 'It's okay. You can come on into the *kampong*.' As we stepped out into the open, Eddie was standing with two villagers. He spoke to them in their own language and they all laughed at us. We asked him why they were laughing and he told us that they knew we were English because the Japs can't grow beards.

The villagers led us to an unoccupied hut and told Eddie we would have to wait there as the head man was coming to speak to us. He came into the hut with two women each carrying a plaited tray with some cut up fruit on banana leaves.

The head man did not speak to us immediately. He appeared to be waiting for someone else to arrive. A young man then came in carrying a small stool and signalled us to stand up, which we did. The head man moved slowly around us, looking carefully at our faces. He was elderly, with grey hair, but still looked very fit, although he walked with a slight limp. After examining us he sat down on the stool and it was then that we noticed that his right leg was extended as though he could not bend it.

He started to speak to us and Eddie replied. The conversation had only been going on for a short time when we realized Eddie was having trouble understanding all that the head man was saying. Eddie broke off the conversation to explain that the language was a mixture of Siamese and Burmese and that it appeared we were on the border of Burma, which was in Japanese hands. Eddie got on first name terms with the head man and although he did not speak Burmese, they were able to converse. When they finally finished, Pit Lok (the head man) had difficulty getting up from his stool. Eddie helped him up and at the same time the young man also stepped forward to help Pit Lok to his feet. For a moment all three stood in a silent group, then burst out laughing. This gave us a boost, although we were still feeling nervous. The young man signalled for us to stand up and the head man left the hut, followed by his companions.

When they had gone Eddie recounted the conversation. He had told Pit Lok we were escaped POWs from the railway construction camps. Neither Pit Lok nor his villagers knew anything about the railway. He had heard rumours that the Japs were in Burma, and that was the way we were heading if we followed the river. He also told Eddie that the rainy season was fast approaching. In fact, we had already had a small taste of it. He warned Eddie that the trails became almost impassable on foot, especially for people in our condition. Small streams became raging torrents and there were leeches, snakes, centipedes and all sorts of other creepy-crawlies.

Pit Lok suggested that as we had come so far, we would be advised to rest up for a while. He could not allow us to stay in his village as that was too dangerous for him and his people, but he would allow us to stay the night and would make sure we were well fed. In the morning he would give us some food and a note to his brother-in-law who lived in a village about a day's march away. His brother-in-law lived in the hill country and would show us a place to hide until we were ready to go on again. That night Pit Lok was as good as his word. We had a feast.

It was obvious the villagers were curious about us and so Eddie suggested that we go outside and let them see what we looked like. We must have looked frightful with our beards and matted hair. Our beards seem to fascinate them as I can't remember ever seeing a native Siamese or Malayan with a beard.

That night we slept better than we had slept for weeks. The next morning we went to the river to try and freshen up and make ourselves presentable. Although I had managed to hang on to my metal army comb my hair was so thick and matted that it was impossible to get the comb through it.

Two girls came to the hut bringing breakfast: two trays with some rice rissoles, which seemed to consist mainly of rice and spiced vegetables that had been fried in oil. We found them very tasty. As soon as we had eaten and had some hot tea, Pit Lok appeared with the young man who had visited us the previous evening. He introduced him as his son. Pit Lok's son was carrying two bags made of plaited palm leaves with food for the journey. Pit Lok also gave Eddie a thin piece of bamboo with a rolled up piece of paper in it, which was the message to his brother-in-law. He told Eddie we would know when we were near his brother's *kampong* as we had to cross a bamboo bridge about ten minutes before we entered it.

When we came out of the hut it seemed as though the whole village had turned out to see us off. We were so grateful to them and although we had nothing to give them, Eddie gave a little speech of thanks. It was then that I had an inspiration and started to sing, 'For they are jolly good fellows, for they are jolly good fellows,' and all the others joined in. As we marched off in true military style all the kids followed us clapping and laughing.

Pit Lok had pointed out the trail we were to take, which seemed to be well-used. It led us in a completely different direction to our river track. It was wide and dry and we were able to walk barefooted. By this stage I was tying my boots together with some of the twine I had found in a deserted village. My sandals were still in reasonable condition but I was loathe to wear them as I hoped that when we reached civilization I would have something decent to put on my feet.

As we walked along the track we noticed dry dust that bore the imprint of bicycle tyre marks. This frightened us as we knew that the Japs rode bikes through the jungle. We kept as quiet as possible. This paid off as the leading man stopped suddenly and raised his hand as a sign of warning. We all heard the sound of voices coming towards us. By now we were experts at getting off the tracks and disappearing into the jungle. Within a few moments we heard a group of men talking to each other as they passed by. Eddie edged his way nearer the path to sneak a look. After they had passed he waved to us to have a quick look. By the time I got to the path they had disappeared but I was told that there were about six natives (Burmese?) pulling a cart similar to a rickshaw, with bike tyres on it. So ended the mystery of the bike tyres and that eased our fears.

After this, we stopped to eat. We opened the bags and found that there were several small parcels of food wrapped up in palm leaves. These were a pre-cooked rissole and we decided to share out a small portion of each so that we all had a taste. It was tasty and spicy. To make the break as short as possible we made do with drinks of cold water from our water bottles.

Remembering that Pit Lok had said that the next village was about a day's walk away, we pushed on until quite late in the evening, which was unusual for us as we liked to be off the track and secure well before sunset. We finally decided that to go any further would be foolish, so we found an open space a few yards off the track that we thought was fairly safe.

We dived into the bags once again and found they contained more parcels of cooked food and a larger parcel had some satays in it, enough for one each. We were really living à-la-carte! We did not bother to light a fire before settling down to sleep and again just drank water from our water bottles.

I don't know how long I had been asleep when I was awakened by an itching on my forehead. When I felt it I had about three bumps. As I lay there I could hear the high pitched whining buzz of mosquitoes around my head. Very soon we were all awake and spent a really bad night doing our best to keep ourselves covered.

Morning came and we couldn't move off fast enough. We were all a bit worried as we thought that maybe we had lost our way and missed the village. After about ten minutes we heard the sound of running water and moments later saw the bamboo bridge across the river. The river was quite large, about 40ft across. The bridge was a suspension bridge built entirely of bamboo and vines; the deck wide enough to take the handcart that we had seen on the trail. Tied to one of the supports was a notice with something written on it in Siamese. Eddie was not able to read the language and so we all joked about what it said. The ideas ranged from, 'Two bob to go across', to, 'One at a time, please', to, 'No fat men allowed'. We never did find out.

We crossed the bridge cautiously and held a short debate on how we should enter the village. We were all of the opinion that Eddie had taken enough chances and that this time we would all go in together. A few yards further on the track opened out into the *kampong* and we saw several people, mostly women and children. They saw us, the children screamed, and they all disappeared into their huts. Within a very short space of time we were surrounded by a group of men who looked quite threatening. Although only armed with sticks and cudgels they still looked dangerous. Eddie spoke to them and showed them the bamboo cylinder with the message inside it. One of the men took it and went inside a large hut. We waited anxiously to see what was going to happen. He soon came back and motioned to Eddie to follow him, signalling for us to sit down. The villagers seemed to relax and started talking amongst themselves.

One of the villagers came over and asked, 'You are English soldiers?' He asked us if we came from Singapore, then surprised us by saying that he had been in Singapore just before the Japanese invasion, but had managed to get out before the city was taken. He also said that some of the men who lived in these jungle *kampongs* had fled from the cities because of the Japs' cruelty to their families. We, in turn, told him of our escape and so we thought that we had found a friend. He asked us where we had escaped from but we could not tell him as we ourselves didn't know the location of the camp. We explained that we had heard the Japs often mentioning Chiang Mai. He said that he thought it would have been Songkrai No. 2 Camp. I can't guarantee either location or the spelling as he could only speak English but not write it. We also told him that we had started out with the intention of getting into China. He then told us, the same as Pit Lok, that we were heading for Burma.

Eventually Eddie came back and told us that the head man said the same as Pit Lok. As far as he knew there were no Japs in the area, but he would not risk having us in the village. He also warned us that the wet season was approaching and we would be foolish to try to go on. Not too far away from his village was a large cave that his men sheltered in if they had to spend a night in the jungle. We could live there quite safely. There was also a deserted *kampong* that we could visit that still had some food growing. The head man didn't tell Eddie why the *kampong* was deserted. We all thought that question was best left unanswered. We would be allowed to stay the rest of the day and sleep the night in his village, but the next morning one of the villagers would act as a guide and take us to the cave. He also warned us to keep out of sight as much as possible while we were in the village as strangers did pass through and he thought it best not to be careless.

The villagers were kind to us and fed us. It seemed that each family donated something cooked and ready for us to eat or drink. We slept under one of the huts on stilts and at first light one of the villagers came to take us to the cave. The man who spoke English had taken our plaited bags the previous night and the man who came to take us to the cave had brought them back to us full of food. We found out it was near the end of August. It took about four hours to reach the cave. I have no doubt that had our guide been alone he would have done it in half the time, but we were still not used to jogging along jungle tracks. The track was obviously a less-used one.

111

In fact, at times, it was overgrown and our guide had to hack the undergrowth away. He spoke no English and the only conversation was between him and Eddie. Again, it seemed they were having a little difficulty understanding each other. Eddie explained to us that the Siamese our guide was speaking was a kind of border language.

We came upon the cave quite suddenly. We heard the sound of running water and the track skirted a stream. There was a small clearing with a steep bank on the other side of the stream and on top of the bank was a row of smallish trees. We climbed up the bank and, on going through the trees, saw the large cave. On looking around, we saw that we had come to a great cliff face.

Here we were, right in the middle of the jungle, and in front of us was a cliff that would not have been out of place in Dover – it was even made of white limestone. Our guide did not seem inclined to hang about and after we had all shown our appreciation he left us to explore our new home.

Chapter 17

The Cave

The cave was large in the front and went deep into the cliff; a man could stand there comfortably We could see it had been used as there were the remains of a bamboo sleeping platform. One of the boys said that if we put a cross on the platform it would be like a church. On closer inspection we found a smaller cave next door, hidden by a large boulder. Both caves had openings which probably led underground, but none of us had any inclination to go caving, especially without lights.

The stream was ice cold, coming from somewhere high up the cliff face, so we thought it was safe to drink. The cave entrance was screened by trees and this made us feel more secure. The guide had pointed out the track that led to the deserted *kampong* the head man had mentioned. We found plenty of dry firewood around the cave and soon had a fire going and something to eat.

Recently Jimmy had started to complain about stomach pains and seemed less and less inclined to eat anything. He wanted to drink all the time. We knew he was really ill. We had no idea what was wrong and so just made him as comfortable as possible. We cut some twigs and branches off the trees to make him a soft bed and gave him an extra blanket. The next morning he was sweating one minute and shivering the next. When he became delirious we knew he had malaria or dengue fever. We hoped and prayed that he would be able to fight the fever but after two days he died. We surmised he had caught the fever the night we had been so badly bitten by mosquitoes.

Burying him was a problem. The only thing we had to dig with was our trusty machete. We tried to dig a grave in two or three places but the ground was as hard as iron. Down by the stream I'd noticed a couple of sickly looking banana plants growing just off the path. I suggested we try digging there. The ground was much softer

113

and so we managed to dig a hole about 4ft deep. We laid Jimmy to rest with his knees bent up so it looked as though he was curled up in bed. After we filled in the grave, we surrounded it with pieces of white stone to mark the spot. We said a prayer or two for him but we were all saddened by the fact that we could do little to save him.

After the burial we decided to explore further afield. Soon we heard the sound of water. From a high bank we stood looking down on a wide, fast-flowing river. There in front of us was a bamboo suspension bridge, which looked as if it would collapse if even a cat walked across it. The walkway was one bamboo pole about 4in or 5in in diameter. This was held in place by poles tied underneath and slung on thick vines spanning the river so that they formed a series of V-shaped supports. Thin vines tied the whole structure together. The bridge was about 20ft above the river and the idea of crossing it scared us. Fred, being the lightest, volunteered to go first. He very carefully made his way on to the bridge. All seemed okay until he got about half-way across, then the bridge started swinging. We could see he was terrified and called out to him to stand still until the bridge stopped swaying. Soon he was able to cross safely. Once Fred had gone across we all followed him very cautiously, one at a time.

Once across we breathed a sigh of relief. The track was well defined and so we decided to take a chance and see where it led. The guide had told us the deserted *kampong* was about half a day's journey away from the cave. From previous experience we knew that half a day could mean anything from four hours to nearly a whole day. Although the track was overgrown in places and we had to chop away some undergrowth, we found it fairly easy to follow. Fortunately, there were no branching paths to confuse us. After about two hours we started to climb a steep hill. It seemed a never-ending climb.

Once again we heard the familiar sound of running water and the path started to skirt a stream. Around the bend we reached the deserted *kampong*. It looked derelict; although the huts were still standing, they looked very old and uncared for. But we soon realized that it was quite large. Eddie suggested we concentrate on finding any fruit trees or vegetables and, although the jungle had done its best to strangle everything, we found wild jackfruit, mangoes, pawpaw, sweet potatoes, corn cobs, and a remarkable tomato vine that had loads of cherry-sized tomatoes on it. We also found lemons and limes, and had we known more about food crops we would have probably have found more root crops, like tapioca and sago. We had taken a couple of backpacks with us and, after tasting some of the tomatoes and fruit, we began to collect supplies to take back to camp. Ian reminded us that if we took too much it may go rotten, so better to leave as much on the trees as possible and come back for more when we needed it. Once we were satisfied with what we had gathered we headed back to the cave, and we made it just before dark.

We now concentrated on making the cave more habitable. There were still plenty of clumps of bamboo about and after spending about three hours taking it in turns to sharpen our machete (*parang* in Malayan) on a wet rock, we started to cut some bamboo to make a new sleeping platform. Up until this time we had been very cautious about making too much noise, but now we were feeling secure we felt we could live fairly normally.

When we had first arrived, the jungle had been quiet with just the odd bird noise. As the days passed we heard more noises, as though we were being watched. One morning we were awakened by loud screeching noises up in the tall trees near the cave. We saw a band of grey long-armed monkeys swinging from branch to branch above us. From then on we saw them all the time and, although they never came too near us, they didn't seem afraid, even when we were chopping bamboo.

Our new sleeping platform was far more comfortable than trying to find a piece of level ground to lie on. The fire was no problem as we found plenty of fuel to keep it going day and night. We no longer felt obliged to boil our drinking water as we had tried drinking straight from the stream and suffered no ill effects.

All too soon we were running out of food, which necessitated another hazardous trip across the river to the deserted *kampong*. We were not looking forward to the journey as there had been intermittent rain and even the area around the cave had become muddy. The first part of the journey was fairly comfortable, but on the climb over the hill we slipped and slid and grabbed for handholds. It was exhausting. When we reached the *kampong*, I decided to look around the huts, and in one I found a paddy-pounder that was quite workable. I baled out as much water from the rice bowl as I could, and went back to tell the others of my find.

Eddie was immediately interested. He said there must be some rice nearby and so we looked in the nearest hut. Sure enough, we found a wooden bin containing quite a lot of unhusked rice. It had a vague musty smell, but it appeared to be quite dry and showed no sign of mildew. Eddie thought it would be edible once we had pounded it. Since the paddy-pounder bowl was very wet it was not possible to de-husk any rice at that time or we'd have just finished up with a soggy mess, so we decided we'd have to wait until another time. We dried out the rice bowl as best we could and covered it with palm leaves to keep out any further rain, then we gathered some more fruit and vegetables and returned to the cave.

We were all young 'townies' and none of us, except Eddie, had any knowledge of living in the jungle. This meant we had to be very careful with our food rationing, as we were always living on the borders of starvation. We decided it was not really necessary for all of us to keep 'going over the hill', as we now called the trip to the *kampong*. We also had to consider the state of the bridge. We were in no fit state to even attempt repairs and if it collapsed we would have no way of crossing the river.

One day Eddie, Taffy and Joe volunteered to go and see if they could get some rice. They left early in the morning and returned about midday the following day with a good quantity of rice. It turned out to be very husky, but we found that by immersing it in water most of the husks and dust floated to the top and we could drain them off. In any case, we had been told that husky rice had more food value.

I, in company with two or three of the others, now had what we called the 'shivers'. For no apparent reason you'd start to shiver violently and the only thing you could do was to lie down and roll up in a blanket so that you kept as warm as possible. Mine was bad and even cold water brought it on. We tried to keep ourselves clean by washing in the river but just touching the cold water started me shivering badly. Even today I don't relish cold showers.

There is nothing very interesting about eking out an existence living in a cave, but we did have some exciting moments. On one occasion we heard voices. Someone was calling out and Eddie said it was a man wanting to talk to us. He went down to the stream and we heard them talking for a few minutes, then Eddie reappeared, accompanied by men from the village we had visited on our way to the cave. They had come because the stream ran into a stretch of fairly deep, clear, calm water and it was a breeding ground for a species of freshwater fish. These men came to catch the fish just before the rainy season, as once the rains set in all fish would be washed down into the big main river and they would lose them. The villagers asked Eddie if we would like to go and watch them fishing by torchlight that night. They had brought their own food and shared some very tasty rice cakes and other morsels with us.

In the evening I followed the stream. I was anxious as I did not want to get the shivers at night-time. Perhaps the excitement boosted my blood pressure though, as my concerns did not eventuate. After a short walk we could see a stretch of open water, almost like a miniature lake. It was here they were going to fish. By this time it was almost dark.

When the men had mentioned torchlight fishing we, in our ignorance, expected them to use battery operated torches. But after waiting until it was fully dark they produced some old-fashioned torches on a stick, made with coconut fibre, or dried palm leaves, dipped in oil or kerosene. They lit the torches and the two men holding them stayed at the point where the creek ran into the pond. Two other men with torches went to the far end of the pond. The other four men then spread out from bank to bank holding a large net that reached across the pond. They began to walk steadily forward followed by the two men with torches. As they came towards us we could see the gleam of jumping fish in the net. Finally, they reached our end and gathered up the net, hauling it out of the water. The net was filled with fish and we even saw some eels. One of the men put a few handfuls of fish into a bag made of sacking and gave them to Eddie with instructions on how to make a fish stew. They then guided us back to our cave. Eddie told us that the men would salt the fish and they would last a long time.

Our expertise was more limited. We selected the largest of the fish, about the size of a medium herring, and roasted them two or three at a time. We found they were quite edible, although very bony. It took a long time to cook and eat them but that just prolonged the pleasure. The smaller fry we put into the pot and boiled with some salt, which made the bones easy to remove. We then mixed the fish with our rice. Today I would probably think it revolting, but after starving for a week it was like cordon bleu.

Shortly after the fishing expedition the rains came and we spent most of the time huddled round our camp fire. We had had the good sense to stockpile as much wood as we could find in anticipation of spending a long period in the cave. We were also eking out food very carefully as none of us was in a fit state to undertake any sort of journey in the wet conditions. Eddie, Bernard and I had tried to go back to the occupied village hoping to get some supplies, but after two or three hours we turned back.

All of us were exhausted and had found several leeches, swollen with our blood, clinging to us. This was my first experience of leeches. I had been told never to pull a leech off as its jaws can rip your skin and cause bad bleeding. The best way to get rid of them is to apply heat, such as a burning cigarette or a red hot ember of wood. Once when I got back to camp I found three on me, one on each leg and one on my upper arm. I tried the burning ember trick and within a few seconds the filthy things dropped off. Fortunately, they were quite small; some can grow to 3in or 4in.

One morning we again heard voices. Some men were calling out to us but we did not show ourselves. Eddie whispered that he didn't understand the language but he was sure it wasn't Japanese. We wondered if they were friend or foe. All went quiet and we hoped they had gone but the voices started again and they appeared to be having a discussion. We went into the small cave behind the rock to try and hide. In a few moments two men appeared at the top of the path to the cave and stood looking around. They saw our fire and scant belongings and knew the cave was occupied. We heard them calling out and soon there were seven of them, the same number as us.

They started to look around. We all thought that they may try to steal what few belongings we had. At a signal from Eddie we decided to show ourselves in a threatening manner. We all stepped out from behind the boulder together. They were surprised to see us. Eddie spoke first and then the two men who had first appeared began to speak. There was lots of talking and sign language and all appeared amicable.

Finally, they left. Eddie explained that they were Burmese men who were going to work in a village he thought was called Chon Dow. He had also heard our cave called the Jam Bhat cave. I cannot guarantee the authenticity of these names or the spelling as I have never been able to find either of them on a map. One other thing he had heard was the mention of Japanese soldiers. This rather scared him as he thought that the men may be going to work for the Japs.

During the rainy season our stream had become a muddy river and the river under the bamboo bridge had become quite a lot bigger. Within a few days of the visit from the Burmese men it was obvious that the worst of the rain was over and we should think about moving on. None of us relished the idea but we knew we could not stay in the cave forever.

Eddie, Taffy and Joe volunteered to go over the hill to the deserted *kampong* to see if there was any food left. While they were there they would also explore the track on the other side of the *kampong*, as we had never been further than the village exit. Eddie thought it possible that the Burmese men had come that way. This left Bernard, Ian, Fred and me back at the cave. When the others returned we would go to the occupied village to see if they could help us in any way. Eddie, Taffy and Joe left in the morning with a small amount of food and we settled down to await their return.

Chapter 18

Recaptured

The morning was clear and fine. We stoked up the fire, measured out our small ration of food and cooked breakfast. Suddenly we heard a voice say loudly, 'Hands up and don't look around.' I was so surprised that my first reaction was to do just that, to look around. I was going to do more when the voice said, 'Keep still, don't move.'

A Japanese soldier appeared in front of us and the voice said, 'Hand over your weapons.' We just sat there petrified, not moving a muscle. The soldier stood there looking at us with his rifle pointed in our direction. Again, the voice said, 'Hand over your weapons.' We all looked at each other and, more or less in unison, said, 'We haven't got any weapons.' Our only weapon was the *parang* and Eddie had taken it with him.

The voice then said, 'Stand up and walk slowly to the wall of the cave and don't turn round.' We did this and stood staring at the cave wall. I don't remember feeling fear as such, but do remember thinking, 'I've gone through all this and now I'm going to be shot in the back.' The next thought I had was about my Mum and Dad and Margaret, my wife. I thought, 'What a way to die, they'll never know what happened to me.'

We must have stood there for four or five minutes and could hear people moving around, probably looking for weapons. The voice then said, 'Put your hands down and behind your backs.' This we were glad to do so as mine were aching badly. I felt someone behind me tying my hands together.

The next order was, 'Turn around and face me.' We turned around and saw a Japanese officer complete with sword, a corporal, a quite well-dressed dark-skinned civilian and a group of other villagers, one with a rifle and the others with pointed sticks.

The voice, we found out, came from the civilian, who told us to sit down. He said he was Burmese and an interpreter. We were to speak through him to our Japanese captors. The first question was why were there only four of us when they had been told seven? We were wide awake enough to be careful how we answered. I said the other three men had gone off and left us.

The interpreter said, 'Ah, you have a disagreement.'

Of course we said, 'Yes, a very bad one.' He seemed quite satisfied with our explanation and jabbered away to the officer. He then asked where we came from and we all tried to tell him at the same time who we were and where we had escaped from. We also told him that we had no idea where we were at the time we had escaped. Once again he spoke to the Jap officer and I twice heard something that sounded like Songkrai No. 2 Campo.

After several other questions, I said, 'One of our men, Jimmy, died.' He said this to the officer who immediately wanted to see the grave. We took them to where we had buried Jimmy and were surprised. The officer spoke to us in English and said, 'You English Christians?' Pointing to the grave, he said, 'No cross, you make one.'

We then went back to the cave and, once again, were told to sit down. I was finding it very uncomfortable with my hands tied behind my back and asked if it was necessary for us to be tied up as we were unarmed and in no fit state to run away.

The interpreter spoke to the officer for a few moments and he said that if we all promised on our honour not to escape, we could be untied. We agreed instantly. Once we were untied the officer pointed to our pile of wood and said to use some creeper to make a cross for Jimmy's grave. Fred did that, and then went with the Japanese soldier to place it on the grave. The officer then made us douse the fire and pack up our meagre belongings.

We left the cave, with one of the villagers leading the way and the soldier behind him. We followed, with the interpreter and the officer next and then, in the rear, the other villager. We got back to the main track and expected that we would go back the way we had come, but instead turned in the opposite direction. We guessed we were heading for Burma. We walked for hours. The guards and the villagers set up a cracking pace and if any of us slowed down we got poked with a stick or yelled at. I was on the point of collapse when suddenly we found ourselves in a village. We were shown to a hut and the interpreter said we would spend the night there. We were

121

exhausted and hungry. My sandals were starting to fall to pieces and my feet were very sore. I call it a hut, but it was more of a bamboo open-sided structure, raised about 4ft off the ground on stilts, with a short ladder to enter it.

The officer, interpreter and the others all disappeared and left the Jap soldier sitting on the ground at the foot of the steps to guard us. We settled down on the bamboo floor which was covered with a couple of woven mats, which made it comfortable. It got dark and, although miserable and hungry, we were quickly asleep.

Within a few hours a voice called out, 'English soldiers wake up.' We looked out to see several fires had been lit around the village. Standing by the steps were two men, one with a hurricane lamp and the other with a large tray of food. One man put the lamp on the floor and the other pushed the tray of food forward and said in passable English, 'You have plenty food and good sleep, tomorrow have long way to go.' We tucked into the food, which was fried garnished rice with small pieces of either pork or chicken in it.

A while later the interpreter came to the hut and asked if we had finished eating. He then reminded us of our promise not to run away and took the lamp. We settled down for the night with no guard. If we had so desired, and been stupid enough, we could have walked back into the jungle.

The next morning we were awake early. The tray was replenished, this time with rice rissoles and patties. Instead of hot drinks we were given cold lime juice which we found refreshing. The officer, the guard and the interpreter came to the hut to collect us. As we walked through the village we could not see any women or children, only men. This time we were only accompanied by our three captors; the villagers were local and stayed at home.

This time we were not so rushed and although my feet were sore I was able to keep going without too much discomfort. Although we stopped for several short breaks, no food was produced. Our captors smoked cigarettes and drank water. The drinking of water bothered us as we still had memories of the cholera epidemic at the camp. We tried to speak to each other several times, but each time the officer would bark out, 'No speak'.

We kept going and reached another village, similar to the last one, but this time some large mats had been spread out on the ground. We were invited to sit down near a fire and were very glad to do this as the nights had become cold. Very soon, plates of food were brought and although ours was placed separately from the guards we all ate together. After we had finished eating, the guards and interpreter spoke to someone who we thought was the head man and he pointed to a hut on stilts. The interpreter told us to pick up the mats we had been sitting on and lay them out underneath the hut as that was where we would sleep. The officer and soldier would be above us in the hut.

Any orders were relayed to us through the interpreter. The Japanese soldier spoke only to his officer and to our ears most of what he said consisted of *ai* (yes), and obeying orders. I knew that the officer understood some English. I remembered his remark about us being Christians and making a cross.

Once again, the weather was fine, the track was well-used and we were making good progress. At last the officer gave the order to halt. We sat in a small clearing and the interpreter and the officer exchanged a few words. The officer was very pleased with our behaviour and if we wished we could talk to each other. We started to chat among ourselves and the officer interrupted us by saying, 'You all English, no Australians?' This took us by surprise and we said we were all English.

The officer's curiosity had got the better of him and he asked our ranks, names and before long we were having quite an informal chat. The Japs produced some cigarettes and the soldier lit one and passed it to Ian, motioning that he should pass it around for us all to have a few puffs each.

In that short interlude things had changed. We had a short discussion among ourselves as to how we should address the officer. The interpreter called him 'Master', such as, 'Master says stop,' or, 'Master says hurry,' but we did not agree to that, neither did we agree on 'Sir'. Finally, we decided that as he was the boss we would ask the interpreter if we could call him 'Number One'. We explained what we would like to do and he agreed to translate our wishes to the officer. The interpreter launched into a torrent of Japanese and we could hear, 'Number One', mentioned several times and, *'ichi may'* (one man), quite often. It appeared to us that he was making a bit of a hash of his explanation. Finally, the officer spoke to us in English and said, 'Why you call me Number One?'

We explained, 'In England anyone who is the top man or in charge, someone who is the best, is always called Number One. We think you are a good man and so we want to call you Number One.'

This was good old-fashioned flattery and we managed to convey it to him without the aid of the interpreter. He was pleased and from then on he became Number One.

The Japanese soldier had no intention of being left out and, pointing to himself, said two or three times, 'Yamoto'. Of course, we were only too pleased to repeat, 'Yamoto,' several times. He was pleased with that. The officer, through the interpreter, told us that had we not been recaptured we would have died or been murdered as we were heading for dangerous hill country. It seemed that even the Jap soldiers were very wary in this part of Thailand.

Night followed day followed night and we stopped at several villages. We were treated well and benefited from the food we were given. My biggest problem was that my footwear was now completely worn out and my feet were in a dreadful state. I had been reduced to tearing my blanket into strips to bind around my feet to give them some protection. But it seemed that after only an hour of walking the strips were reduced to flapping rags.

Eventually we came to the bank of a river and the path skirted around a large rocky bluff. As we approached the rocks it became clear that it was some kind of quarry. There were smashed rocks and there was sharp gravel all over the place. The Japs, the interpreter, Ian and the others all had good or reasonable footwear. I, on the other hand, was practically barefooted but had no option but to cross the rocks with the others. After walking for only a few yards I knew I was in deep trouble; each step was agonizing.

Somehow I made my way across, but tears were streaming down my face. I think the worst part was that none of my companions tried to help me. In fact, Ian was more concerned that I was letting the Japs see me in distress. Finally, I made it to the smooth ground and it felt wonderful. A very short time after that we arrived at a village situated almost on the riverbank. We were allowed to rest and I was able to bathe my badly cut feet.

Later in the day the interpreter visited us to tell us that in the morning we would continue our journey by boat. Number One had also told the interpreter to tell us that he thought we were brave men to have escaped from the railway camp. A lot of men had died there, including some Japanese. One other item of interest was that it was the party of Burmese labourers that had given our position away. There was a reward of $60 per head on any white man found in the jungle. I was sure that the interpreter may have had something to do with them as he kept asking us about the other missing men.

I was delighted to hear that for the time being at least we had finished walking. Apart from the cuts from the stones, my feet festered from debris on the track as it was full of thorns. All I could do was to try and pull them out with my fingers, or just wait until they popped out on their own.

After our usual small ration of rice for breakfast we were escorted to a landing stage where our river transport waited. There were two boats tied up. They were sailing vessels and obviously used for river transport as they were loaded up with goods covered over with mats and tarpaulins. There were two crewmen aboard each boat. The men in the first boat signalled for two of us prisoners to step aboard. It seemed that Bernard and Ian wanted to stay together, so Fred and I boarded the other boat together and Yamoto came on board with us. Bernard, Ian, the interpreter and Number One boarded the other larger boat and we set off down the river.

Our boat was not built to carry passengers but we managed to make ourselves comfortable by sitting in a well in the stern, with our backs resting against some cargo. The crew hoisted the sail and, as the river had a fairly fast flowing current and we were heading downstream, there didn't seem much for them to do except to steer the boat with a large oar at the stern.

For a while I gazed at the jungle slipping by. I looked across at Yamoto and saw that he had made himself comfortable with his rifle across his bent knees. Fred was sitting beside me and we were both surprised when Yamoto raised his hand in greeting and said, 'Goodaga, jhato English asta awardi.' The 'goodaga' was the Japanese version of 'good', as 'speedo' is the Japanese version of 'hurry'. The rest was in Japanese and meant, 'Good tomorrow English finish.' Exactly what he meant by that we couldn't fathom, but he was obviously pleased about it. We gave him a smile and a wave in return and in about five or ten minutes our guard was asleep.

At about noon I could smell wood smoke drifting back to where we were sitting and not long afterwards one of the crew came and offered each of us a bowl of food, complete with chopsticks. It was fried rice with pork and a chilli sauce. It was a tasty meal and I managed to use the chopsticks. Yamoto carefully picked out the meat and then putting the bowl to his lips proceeded to shovel the rice into his mouth, making animal-like noises while doing so. A short time later we were given some bowls of hot tea. Had we been offered a cold drink I would have refused it, as I noticed that any water was from a bucket that had been hauled out of the river.

Later in the day we came to a landing stage with a single wooden building on the riverbank. Our boat made for the landing stage and tied up. Number One's boat arrived almost before we had time to disembark. The interpreter told us we would be spending the night in the hut as the river was too fast flowing and dangerous to navigate at night. The crew started to cook the evening meal. It was then that I realized the smoke I had smelt earlier in the day had come from a fireplace on board the boat. The food they served up was almost identical to the midday meal, but was still welcome. After the meal, everyone sat around talking. Ian told us that Number One had been asking them about Jimmy and had somehow got the idea that Jim had been the leader of the party. Ian felt that it was best to let him think that was the case.

Finally, it was time to retire for the night and the crewmen went aboard their boats to sleep. Our party went into the wooden building and spread ourselves out on the floor. There was no door and Yamoto laid his sleeping mat across the doorway, presumably to guard us.

Probably because I had slept a lot during the day I couldn't settle at all. Later, a bright moon came up and shone on the river, through the doorway and right into the hut making it even more difficult to sleep. After tossing and turning I was just about to nod off when I heard a 'plop' near my head. I turned to see what it was and in the moonlight I could see something moving about. I was wide awake in an instant. It was some sort of snake. Of course I panicked and, jumping up, started shouting that there was snake in the hut. Within seconds everyone was on their feet, not knowing what I was yelling about. Yamoto was standing in the doorway with his rifle at the ready and the interpreter was jabbering away in his own language. I could see the snake was moving and all I could say was, 'There's a snake on the floor.'

The interpreter then understood and rushed out to the landing stage to call the crew. One of them came, carrying a sack. He carefully went up to the snake, threw the sack over it, scooped it up and took it outside. He then spoke to the interpreter and they both started to laugh. The interpreter came and explained that it was one of the harmless species that live in palm thatched roofs and feed on lizards. We were very relieved.

The next morning we were not spoken to at all except to tell us to board the boats. We wondered why there was no breakfast. The boats pushed off from the jetty and we were on our way once again. We were facing the stern of the boat so we could not see ahead. I began to notice that the boat was going faster and the man on the oar at the rear was working harder. The second man had disappeared and I stood up to see what was going on. He was standing at the bow with a long heavy pole in his hands and straight ahead was a gorge. I could see the water rushing through it. I said to Fred that he'd better have a look at what was ahead. We had only been standing a few moments when the steersman yelled at us to sit down.

Suddenly we heard the rushing water. The boat was bounding along and we could feel it hitting rocks and bouncing up and down. In moments we, too, were being bounced about. Both Fred and I were scared and Yamoto was talking to himself. I think he was as terrified as we were. We could see the tall cliffs looming above us and the boat seemed to be tearing along at great speed. The banging and bumping went on for ages and then gradually the noise abated and we were once again in calmer water.

About an hour or so later we began to see other boats plying the river. We were approaching a large town. The crewmen guided our boat through a maze of other boats and tied up to a small landing stage. Yamoto signalled us to remain on the boat and he got off to wait for Number One's boat, which appeared a few minutes later. Once they were both tied up we were allowed ashore with Ian and Bernard.

We barely had time to speak before a covered truck appeared and two Japanese soldiers got out and spoke to Number One. There was a lot of bowing and ceremony going on and finally the interpreter told us that we were to get into the truck. The Japs with the truck were our new masters. They wore a different uniform to Yamoto and, instead of rifles, they had revolvers strapped to their waists. One of the Japs got into the cab, the other one climbed into the back with us and off we went. One of us started to speak, but immediately the Jap made a grab for his pistol. It was obvious that we were not to talk.

Chapter 19

Moulmein – now Mawlamyine

After a short drive we arrived at a large house and drove through a pair of entrance gates. It appeared to have been some sort of government building in peacetime, as it had a coat of arms over the entrance. We were not taken into that building, however, but to a smaller one that was similar in appearance to a police station. Once inside, we were told to stand to attention as we were now prisoners. After a few minutes another Japanese appeared and, in English, said that we would be locked up for a long time. We were led away to yet another building and, once inside, found it was a large room with a wooden cage about 10ft square built into its centre. We were put into the cage and left. It was now late afternoon. We were all feeling miserable and I imagined us being shut up in the cage until we starved to death. We were now in the hands of the dreaded *Kempeitai* (the Japanese Military Police). I don't even remember if we had any food that night. The room was quite dark as it seemed to have louvred shutters at the windows, which were partially closed.

The next morning two men came and unlocked the cage. They took us to an ablution shed, which had showers and running water. We had to strip off and they watched us while we showered. We had to leave our clothes and they gave us a small towel each to dry ourselves. Afterwards, we were squirted with some strange-smelling white powder from a puffer pack. Of course, later in life, I realised that we had been sprayed with DDT to kill our fleas – we were infested with them: in our beards, our hair and our clothes.

We were each given a pair of light cotton underpants and taken out into the open air, where we sat on some stools. The men cut our beards and hair and then ran the clippers all over our faces and heads. They finished by presenting us each with a safety razor. Each washbasin had a piece of bright steel for a mirror. I couldn't believe my eyes when I saw a gaunt face with white powdery looking skin and a head encrusted with a thick layer of dandruff. I looked like a warmed-up corpse, which I suppose I was. Up until then I hadn't looked at the others but when I did I barely recognized any of them. The Japs didn't give us any soap but we were only too glad to be able to have a proper wash. Although there was only cold water, it had been in the pipes long enough to warm up and it felt heavenly.

Once this was all done, the guards took us back to our cage and shut us in. The shutters were opened to let the daylight in. Things were getting better all the time. We were given some food and water. Finally, we were brought some clean clothing: shorts and a top of a thick cotton material. This was a help as it got quite cold at night.

The next day we were taken, one at a time, to be interrogated. I was the first to go. It is very difficult to describe the feeling when someone appears at the door of a cage with a pistol and motions you to come with them on your own. A distinct chill ran down my spine when I accompanied him to an office and was told to sit down, especially as it was all done in sign language. The room had a desk, some chairs and several filing cabinets. On one of the filing cabinets perfumed joss sticks were burning.

The guard who sat waiting with me suddenly jumped up, motioning for me to do the same. A very smart officer came into the room, sat down at the desk and, as usual, took out a packet of English cigarettes. He lit a cigarette and opened a folder that he had brought with him. After looking at it for a minute or so, he started to speak in almost perfect English.

'What is your name?'

'Peter Jackson.'

'Where do you live?'

'England.'

'What city?'

'London.'

He then said, 'You arrived in Singapore in 1942.'

'Yes.'

'What ship were you on?'

'The *Wakefield*.'

'What regiment?'

'I'm not supposed to tell you that.'

'It does not matter. I know all about it.'

He then surprised me by asking if I had any family. I told him about my family.

'Would you like a cigarette?'

I said, 'Yes, please.' He then passed one to me.

'How long were you working on the railway (at Songkrai Camp)?'

I told him about the cholera and how bad the conditions were.

'I understand, but you still escaped from your Japanese masters.' I said it was better than dying in the camp. Whether he was playing me along I don't know, but he appeared to be more friendly.

He then surprised me by saying that he knew all about the American ships landing at Singapore and asked me if I remembered some men selling drinks and pineapples on the docks when I arrived. He told me that he was one of those men, and that in his folder he had the names of all the ships and how many men were on them. 'What do you think of that?' he said. I was dumbstruck.

I can't remember how long the interrogation lasted, but it all seemed very amicable and when it was over I was not taken back to the cage but put in a room with bars on the window. This was so that I was not able to tell the other members of my party what I'd said. Finally, after we had all been interrogated we were put back into our cage. Our stories must have satisfied the Japanese as we were not asked any more questions.

Each morning we were allowed out for a short time to wash and toilet ourselves. The rest of the day, if we needed to go to the lavatory, we had the use of a wooden bucket with a seat on it. Each morning one of us had to carry it out and empty it down a sump in the yard.

We were fed twice a day, morning and evening. I can't say what sort of food it was, but I do know the rations were pitifully small. We had learnt very early in our internment that the Japs believed that no work meant no food; this applied even to their own men. We had been told by some of the guards that sick men were only given half the food of fit men.

After we had been locked up for about three days we were all feeling the need for exercise. We asked to see the interpreter, to find out if there was any work we could do that would give us exercise. Once again, fortuitous circumstances worked in our favour. One evening a guard came in to bring our food and was humming a tune. This, in itself, was surprising as usually it was a very sober occasion, but even more surprising was that it was a tune we knew

130

well, a Glenn Miller song. We more or less unconsciously joined in and somehow we started talking about music. We spoke no Japanese, he spoke no English, but we managed to convey to each other what we meant. One soldier and four English men all demonstrating different instruments must have been a comical sight, all with appropriate sounds and actions.

Beep, beep beep a beep a do – Japanese *clarinetto*
Beep, beep beep a beep a do – English clarinet
Da da da diddy diddy da do – Japanese *trumpetto*
Da da da diddy diddy da do – English trumpet
Dong dong dong ding ding ding – Japanese piano
Dong dong dong ding ding ding – English piano

It seemed that the Japanese names of most of the instruments were the same as the English name with an 'o' or 'ka' on the end. An accordion became a piano *accordianka*, but most stringed instruments had a different name. Of course, we were sensible enough to let our Japanese jazz enthusiast think that the Japanese names were correct. The best part was when we were discussing drums. We were all very enthusiastic over these and had a real jam session.

Somehow we got through to Jazzy, as he became to us, that we would like to speak to the interpreter. The next afternoon the interpreter paid us a visit and we explained our desire to work. He wasn't very impressed with our request and reminded us that we were prisoners of war and, as such, enemies of the Japanese. He went off in a real huff and we thought that was the end of that. But, the next morning we were surprised when a guard came to the cage and unlocked the door. He took us out into the bright sunlight, led us to the front of the large building and pointed to the weeds and grass growing in the gravel drive. We were each provided with a gardening tool of some sort. We could not believe our good luck. We were going to do the same job as the one we had been doing before we escaped from the railway camp.

For about four hours we dug and hoed and raked. Personally, I was beginning to doubt the wisdom of asking for work. The sun was very hot, my feet were still sore from walking in the jungle, and I had no footwear, so working on the rough gravel was very uncomfortable. But from then on we were sent to work every day, until one morning when a Japanese person of rank came into the room and began talking. His voice got louder and his hand was shaking the hilt of his sword. It was obvious that something had gone wrong. That was the last day we were allowed out.

We thought that we would spend the rest of the war in our cage, but one day who should come to visit us but our old friend Number One. We were told that the next day we would accompany Number One somewhere. The Japanese had different names for some places so we were not sure where we were going.

Our prison clothes were taken off us and our own clothes returned; they had been washed and sanitized. Also, our meagre belongings were returned. I was very pleased to get my comb back as my hair was growing very quickly. We started our journey in an open-decked Chevrolet truck which, no doubt, had been captured by the Japs at some time. Number One sat in the front with the driver. A guard, new to us, sat on a box with a cushion on it at the back, and we sat on the metal floor with our backs against the wooden sides of the truck. We were soon to learn that Japanese drivers are completely mad. The road was bumpy. It turned and twisted and we were thrown from side to side. Even the guard struggled not to be thrown onto the floor. Adding to our discomfort was the fact that when the sun came out the metal deck of the truck got so hot we could barely touch it with our hands.

At long last we stopped at what we immediately recognized as a railway camp. We could see men working but before we could take much note of anything we were pushed into a tarpaulin-covered wagon and the door shut, which left us in total darkness. We could hear several Japs moving around, talking, and then we felt the train start to move.

Gradually our eyes got used to the gloom. We could see a lot of cardboard and brown paper on the floor, probably left from parcels the Japanese had opened and hadn't bothered to clear up. We scraped the paper and cardboard into a heap and made ourselves as comfortable as we could. The incessant squeaking and banging of the wheels was deafening and we were still being jerked and bumped about.

One corner of the tarpaulin had come loose and was flapping about letting in some air and flashes of light. I was the nearest to the loose corner and, standing up, cautiously peeped out. Right behind the engine was a wagon with a platform built onto it and sitting on the platform were some Japanese soldiers behind a machine gun. Two trucks away from ours was another the same. It seemed the

132

Japs were prepared for any trouble. Once the others had had a peep we decided it was best to keep our heads down.

After an interminable time we stopped at what sounded like a busy place. More shouts in Japanese and, finally, the door was opened and we were told to come out. We were hustled along a platform and put into a covered truck. As we sped out of the station I saw the sign: Bangkok.

Chapter 20

Bangkok

Our arrival in Bangkok was similar to our reception in Moulmein. After we had dismounted from the truck we were escorted into a large building and made to wait in a reception area until two new guards led us into the inner part of the building. Through heavy wooden doors we entered a very large room filled with three rows of wooden cages: one along each wall and one in the centre. As we walked past, we saw that they were each occupied by one person sitting upright in the cross-legged position.

Soon the guards stopped, unlocked a cage door and motioned for one of us to step inside. After some hesitation and some growled threats from the Japs, Bernard stepped into the cage. We hoped we would be in adjacent cages but had no such luck. I was in a rear cage that was fixed to the wall. The two side walls were of solid construction and the front was made of wooden bars with a barred door. The door had a 4in or 5in gap at the bottom. If I spread out my arms I could touch both walls, so I guessed it was about 6ft wide and about 7½ft long. It contained a wooden bucket with a lid, a blanket and wooden block with a hollow in it that was a headrest for sleeping. There was no mistaking what the bucket was for as the smell was overpowering.

I was sore, tired, hungry and thoroughly miserable. I folded my blanket into a pad to sit on and, leaning my back against the wall, I went to sleep. It seemed only moments had passed when I was woken by a guard banging on the wooden bars and yelling. I was so fed up that I just sat and glared at him. I expected that any minute he would come into the cell to beat me up and I couldn't have cared less.

Suddenly I got the shivers, whether it was nerves or starvation or the cold I don't know, but it was very bad. My teeth were chattering and my whole body was shaking, I just couldn't control myself. I

134

must have looked terrible because the guard gave up yelling at me and disappeared. He came back a short time later with another man and they let me wrap myself up in the blanket and lie down on the floor. In a matter of seconds I was asleep.

I was awakened later by a noise that sounded like metal dishes banging together. It was the sound of food being dished up to my fellow inmates and I anxiously waited to see what would happen to me. I was afraid they would pass me by. Two natives stopped at my cell and pushed one large and one small bowl under my door. The large bowl contained food, the small one hot tea. Instead of chopsticks, the large bowl had a spatula in it, which I found easier to use.

I had recovered from the shivers and, once I had eaten and had the hot tea, felt much better and was able to take stock of my surroundings. There was plenty of daylight in the building as it had a row of tall arched windows along the top of each wall. I could see the sky and the tops of trees, but it was not possible to see out of the windows as they were about 6ft off the floor.

Opposite me I could see the occupant of another cell facing me. He was dressed in white clothes and was not Japanese. I tentatively waved to him, but he just ignored me. He sat in the same position as the other men we had seen: cross-legged, hands on his knees, back straight. In fact, he almost seemed to be in a trance – maybe he was meditating.

The guard wore soft rubber shoes and other than the swish of clothing and padding of feet, there was not a sound. He passed my cell three or four times before it got dark and each time looked in and muttered something: nothing very complimentary, I was sure.

Just before dark some lights were switched on and a bell rang. After that I could hear all around me the sounds of prisoners getting ready to sleep. I rolled myself in the blanket, put my wooden pillow under my head and tried to sleep. Eventually, I found it was better to fold my blanket over the wooden block three or four times and rest my head on it. My feet were cold but at least my head was comfortable.

The next morning a bowl of cold water was pushed under the door with a piece of towelling about the size of a face flannel. The orderly whispered in English, 'Wash face quickly'. I soon understood why, because I scarcely had time to wash the upper part of my body when another man came to take away the bowl. I left the cloth on the side of the bowl but he signalled that I should keep it in my cell. After this a small amount of food was brought around and then, after the bowls were collected, there was nothing to do but sit in silence. It seemed that none of the prisoners were allowed out for exercise. I began to have visions of being shut in this wooden cage for years, dressed in my old clothes, now more or less in rags.

A couple of days later, I heard some Japanese talking quite loudly, which was unusual, then the sound of heavy footsteps, the jangle of keys opening a door and then the footsteps coming to my cage. I stepped out to see Bernard with a Jap soldier. One by one we were let out and then taken outside. We could not talk to each other but knew without speaking how we all felt at being together again. We were taken across the yard to another group of buildings, between which was another wooden cage. Sitting in the cage were three men: Eddie, Taffy and Joe. It was difficult to recognise them at first, they looked so dreadful.

At first we didn't quite know how to react. We remembered we had told the interpreter that we had parted on bad terms. We didn't need to worry though, as the Japs just opened the door and pushed us inside with the usual admonition, 'No speako'. Although we tried to have whispered conversations, they seemed to hear the slightest word and so we had to keep silent.

We had not been there long, when the Japs came back, opened the cage and motioned for all of us to follow them into a building and up some stairs. We found ourselves in a courtroom. Not that I had ever been in a courtroom, but it was just like one in the films. We all wondered what on earth was going to happen next.

A Japanese soldier entered the room and told us we were going to be tried under Japanese military law. He was our interpreter and we could speak to the court through him. A door behind the judge's bench opened and immediately we were told to stand up and bow. Although I was stooped over in a bow, I was still able to see what was going on up on the bench.

One after another four Japanese officers trooped in. The interpreter spoke briefly to the judges and then told us, 'You are charged under Section 7 of the Japanese Army Act with being escaped prisoners of war. You also are charged with failing to do the work allotted to you by his Imperial Highness, the Japanese Emperor.'

Some clever bloke might have trotted out something about the Geneva Convention: that it was considered a prisoner's duty to escape, that POWs should not be made to work on jobs of military importance – which the railway obvious was – and that all POWs should be adequately housed and fed. But the Japanese were not signatories to the Geneva Convention and none of us wanted to be heroic, so we pleaded guilty.

Looking at his notes the interpreter said he had some questions to ask us on behalf of the judges.

'Which one of us was the leader of the party?' was his first question. I can't remember who said it, probably Eddie, but the answer came quick as a flash, 'Oh, he died in the jungle.'

'What was his name?'

'James S'.

'How did he die?'

'Sickness killed him.'

The interpreter translated this to the judges and after a brief discussion turned to us and in a very civilized manner asked if we had anything to say in our defence. We more or less all tried to join in, telling him about the cholera epidemic and the sickness in the camp. He gave us a minute or so and again spoke to the judges.

The judges conferred and finally the one who seemed most senior addressed us in Japanese. He sounded very serious. 'You have been found guilty of wilfully disobeying your Japanese masters. However, we have taken into account the fact that you feared death by disease, and were willing to risk your lives by escaping into the jungle. This shows us that you are brave men. The punishment for your crime is that the leader of your party shall be put to death, but as he has already died in the jungle your punishment will be life imprisonment to be served in Singapore.'

After bowing the officers out, we were taken back to our cage. We would have loved the opportunity to talk about what had happened but no chance presented itself as the Japanese insisted on a strict code of silence. My private thoughts were, 'Thank God. Had Jimmy not been named as the ringleader, the Japs may have picked on one of us survivors.' My other thought was, 'How can I become a life prisoner when I'm already a prisoner of war?' I didn't know it at the time but I was soon to find out.

Our trial and the sentencing had taken place in the morning. We were given a small meal and some hot tea. After this we were taken out two at a time and allowed the pleasure of a five-minute shower. No soap, but the usual face flannel-sized towel. After the shower, the barber had another go with his clippers, carrying on until he was satisfied and I felt as though I had no skin left. All the time he was clipping me, he was making disgusted noises, so heaven knows what he found. When we were cleaned up, our old clothes were disposed of and we were issued with clean ones – a kind of prison garb.

Once back in the cell I felt that things weren't so bad after all. At least I was alive and being fed. It seemed that once the trial was over we had taken on a different status, as the next morning we were taken out for a wash and even allowed ten minutes of exercise under the watchful eye of a guard. This soon came to an end though. One morning we were told we were going on to Singapore. Our prison clothes were taken off us and we were given back our old rags. We were ordered into a covered truck. This time two guards accompanied us in the back of the transport. We sped off through the streets of Bangkok but the two Japs sitting at the rear of the truck obscured any view we may have had of the city.

At the railway station, we were hustled off the truck and put into a waiting room. Our old 'friend' Number One came into the room while the two other Japs stood guard outside. While we had been prisoners, most of us had learnt to speak and understand a little Japanese and we had a faltering conversation with Number One. After a short time, Number One went to the door and spoke to one of the guards. I saw him give the guard some money.

A little later, there was a knock on the door and a native entered carrying a basket. He set it down on a table and we saw it was full of food. Except for two small loaves of bread and a whole cooked chicken, most of it was Thai food and it all tasted delicious. Number One looked on as we were eating and nodded approval when we used our limited Japanese to indicate that we were enjoying the food. Two bottles of cold lime juice had been supplied and were passed around for each of us to take a swig.

After the meal, Number One told us that in about half an hour he would be handing us over to the *Kempeitai* (police) and, in his words, '*No goodaga.*' We felt quite apprehensive. We thanked him as best we could, showing our appreciation by shaking hands in the English fashion. Although he had been our captor, he had treated Ian, Bernard, Fred and myself very kindly, as far as he could. From what little we could understand from Eddie, Taffy and Joe, they had not fared so well when they were caught. But we never really knew

138

what had happened to them because I was never allowed to talk to them again.

Finally, we were taken to a waiting train. According to the station clock it was 6.30pm. It seemed that this time we were to travel in comfort, as we sat in a proper compartment with upholstered seats. I had the good fortune to get a window seat just inside the door. The two guards waited on the platform and only climbed aboard as the whistle blew to signal the train's departure. One guard sat opposite me and the first thing he did was to pull down my blind, so much for a window seat. The other guard took up a position in the corridor. It seemed no time at all after we left Bangkok that the lights came on in the train and it got dark outside.

The guards frequently changed places – one sitting, one standing. With seven men in one compartment who had been well fed, it was inevitable that there was always one or another of us wanting to use the lavatory. Whichever of the guards was on duty would accompany us, all the time moaning at us in Japanese. They made it quite plain that we were objects only worthy of contempt.

The train rattled on and on through the night. I slept fitfully, aware all the time of the Japs in the carriage. If the train stopped or slowed to a crawl, which it frequently did, I could hear the snip of the safety catches being lifted on the guards' revolvers in case one of us made a move to escape.

Morning came, and the Japanese lifted down their haversacks and proceeded to eat a picnic breakfast. They made no attempt to either feed us or give us a drink. Other than the occasional visit to the lavatory we were not even allowed the privilege of exercise.

I had not been feeling good for some days. The shivers seemed to come and go. I was feeling very weak. Life had become one long nightmare. My feet and ankles were still very badly swollen and infected, so I probably had a lot of poison in my system. By the time the train arrived in Singapore I was quite ill, but neither the Japs nor my comrades seemed concerned. We were bundled into a truck and driven to prison.

Chapter 21

Outram Road Prison

Our prison this time had no wooden bars or cages. It was a real prison with a cell door that clanged shut as we were locked in. I was sharing with another member of our party. We went through the usual procedure of being allowed a bucket of water and a facecloth-sized towel to wash with. Back at the cell, I was given a clean set of clothes, a blanket and a wooden *mukral* (pillow). There was the inevitable wooden bucket, accompanied by some toilet paper-sized pieces of newspaper. Unfortunately, the script was in Japanese and there were no pictures, so I couldn't read it. The door of the cell was of thick wood, with large steel hinges and a heavy metal grill at the bottom for ventilation. About 5ft up from the floor an oblong hole with a small shelf was cut into the door, which served as a spy hole and was also used to pass food and clothing through.

All I wanted to do was lie down and go to sleep. I was not a bit interested in my cellmate as, unfortunately, he was the one person I couldn't get on with in our party – and neither was he interested in me. I slept for a while and was woken by the familiar sound of metal dishes clanging. One bowl was plonked on the shelf. My cellmate took it and another one appeared. It was grudgingly passed to me but after one or two tries at eating the food I just couldn't manage it. My cellmate asked if I wanted it and when I said I didn't, within moments it had disappeared.

Later a guard appeared at the hole in the door holding up a piece of cardboard with some numbers on it. He kept repeating the same thing over and over. My cellmate finally understood that I was 610 (*roku aka ju*) and he was 611 (*roku aka juichi*).

A small barred window about 7ft up in the wall let in a little daylight and shortly after dark I heard the Japs start roll call. Each cell was visited and when your number was called you had to answer with a loud, '*Hai*' (yes). When the guard called my number, he couldn't hear me and looked through the slit to see me lying down. I heard the rattle of keys and the cell door was opened. The guards came in and, standing over me a most threatening manner, made me stand up and shout, '*Hai*', at the top of my voice, about six times. I tried to make them understand that I was ill but they didn't want to know.

The next morning we were made to parade outside for our bucket wash and ten minutes of exercise. Somehow I managed to get through that ordeal and back to the cell to lie down. I heard the food being dished out and again, refused to eat. My cellmate scoffed my portion. I slept through most of the day but was aware of the guards looking through the door and probably swearing at me. I couldn't have cared less.

We were fed twice a day, morning and evening. It just so happened that as the evening meal was being dished up I had to get up to go to the lavatory. As the people who were dishing out the food came along I could hear someone speaking in a mixture of Japanese and English. I took a chance and looked out of the hole in the door. I saw a Jap with a white man and two Indians who were carrying a large tray full of dishes of food. The Jap was ticking off the cells as the white man was serving the food. When he got to my cell, my cellmate tried to push me away from the door but I wasn't going to let an opportunity pass to talk to someone in English.

As the man came to the door, I said, 'Can I talk to you?' He spoke briefly to the Jap and, turning to me, asked what I wanted. I told him that I was ill and that I couldn't eat any of the food and was getting weaker and weaker. He spoke to the Jap again, after which he wanted to know what had happened to the other food that had been left for me. My cellmate knew the game was up and confessed that he had eaten it.

When the English speaking server told the Japanese guard what had happened, he let fly at my cellmate with a choice flow of words. The server explained that if people eat their food the guards never believe they are ill. If anyone is sick the usual thing is to return the food uneaten.

Just before roll call, my cellmate was moved out and later that night I was visited by someone who gave me an injection in my upper arm. For the next two or three days I was fed on a liquid diet and given some pills to take. Eventually I got better and was at least able to lead a normal prison life.

I was now in solitary confinement. I had no means of telling the time or the days of the week. Each day was the same with no variation: it began with the ringing of a bell, which meant my blanket was to be folded up into a neat square and my wooden block pillow placed on top of it. The cell door was opened, I stepped out and down two steps onto the floor of the main hall. The guards took us eight at a time out into the prison yard where each man stood in front of a bucket of water and small towel. On a word of command, I'd raise the bucket of water and tip it over my body as a shower. Once the bucket was empty I had to refill it and put it in place for the next man. When the bucket was refilled I was allowed to dry myself.

After washing, I had about ten minutes of exercise. This entailed stretching arms upward, stretching outward, knees bending, touching the toes and so on. All this was done to the count of eight, chanted by the guards and prisoners. Even to this day I sometimes find myself counting *Ichi, Ni, San, Shi, Go, Roku, Shichi, Hachi*. When the exercises were over I was taken back to the cell, locked in and then fed. The food was totally inadequate: the soup was vegetable water with a few unidentified bits of green floating in it, plus a small bowl of rice.

Later in the morning a group of six English and Australian prisoners under the charge of a Jap guard came to collect the slop buckets (*benki*). This party consisted of four men who carried a large tray with handles and two who visited each cell and took out the *benkis*. These were placed on the tray and taken away to be emptied and brought back later. Sometimes when the guard was not too near at hand the *benki*-boys were able to give me small scraps of information.

I learned that the man who was in charge of the Indians who delivered the food was an English Indian Army officer who had refused to command his troops when the Indian Army went over to the Japanese. His sentence was nearly complete and he was due to return to Changi in the near future. I asked about the rest of my escape party, but none of the *benki*-boys knew of them. The whispered conversations were limited to a very few words. Except for these very brief and dangerous exchanges my days were spent in silence.

The cell block was constantly patrolled by a Japanese guard. I estimated that he passed my cell about every fifteen minutes. Since we prisoners were supposed to sit in a lotus position I contrived to be sitting in something like it when I heard the shuffle of his feet as he approached my cell. I never quite knew when I would look at the hole in the door and see a pair of eyes staring back at me.

The evening meal was served, then roll call and, finally, the bed-time bell. As soon as it got dark a light in the ceiling of my cell was switched on and so I was never in darkness, day or night. I used the same technique for sleeping as I did in Bangkok by folding my blanket (*morfu*) over the block (*mukra*) a few times and leaving my legs bare. I also slipped one arm out of the sleeve of my jacket and covered my eyes with it until I went off to sleep. The guards must have disapproved of my way of sleeping as, on several occasions, I was awakened by a banging on the door and some words of dis-approval.

Slowly my health began to improve and I found that I could exercise in the confines of my cell. I tried to keep mentally active by pretending that I was back at school and the teacher was writing on the blackboard. I was always imagining what wonderful food I was going to eat, such as a loaf of new bread with a beautiful brown crust on it. I would cut the loaf in half and smear it with loads of butter. I would then have half a pound of ham off the bone and make a gigantic ham sandwich. I would also dream of cooking bacon, eggs and tomatoes over a camp fire. At one stage I spent ages thinking of all the foreign words that have crept into the English language.

On one occasion I thought that I was due for a beating. I was sitting on my *benki* doing what comes naturally and was folding a piece of paper into the shape of a boat, or flower, or something like that. I was unaware of a Japanese guard watching me through the slot. Suddenly the door was unlocked and the guard burst in. He grabbed the paper off me, lectured me and at the same time, waved his sheathed sword in front of my face. I was terrified.

After about two months I heard voices approaching my cell at a very unusual time. The door was opened and a guard I had not seen before came in with a man who appeared to be a white civilian. He and the guard stood looking at me for a minute or two and then he asked me how I felt. I told him that I felt better than when I had come to the prison. He also asked me if I exercised in the cell. I told him I did.

After a brief conversation with the Japs he told me that one of the *benki*-boys was due to be let out within a day or so and if I wished, I could take his place. If I took the job as a worker I would be entitled

143

to a little extra food. They would give me a trial the next morning. I spent the next few hours in anticipation of being able to get out of my cell and fear that I would be too weak to do the job.

The next morning after breakfast a guard came to let me out of my cell and I found myself in the company of the six *benki*-boys. We marched in an orderly fashion to a part of the prison I had not seen previously. Actually, the only part of the prison that I had seen was between my cell and the exercise yard, so everything I did and saw that morning was completely new to me.

We went through a door into a courtyard. Standing against a wall were three or four large wooden trays with a handle at each corner. Four men stepped forward and, each holding a handle, carried it towards the door. The other two men and I followed them through the door back into the cell block.

The men seemed to have a set routine and the guard was content to let them do their job, other than for a grunt now and again. As they came to each cell the guard opened the door and one of the men went in and carried out the full *benki*, placing it on the tray. The guard was opening two or three doors ahead of us and after the *benkis* had been lifted out was going back to close the cell door. This gave the men a few moments to have a quick whisper to the prisoner in his cell. I had been following along, then the guard demonstrated that I should go into the cells and carry out the benkis.

After the first two or three, I realized this was no easy job. A wooden bucket full of waste can be quite a heavy load. However, I was determined to soldier on. The thought of some extra daily food gave me strength I didn't know I had. While we did the ground floor, I discovered that not all the prisoners were soldiers, nor were they all English. There were also Indian, Chinese and Malays. We then took the full tray back out into the yard, where there was a large concrete sump with a wooden cover over it. It was our job to empty the contents of each bucket down the large hole. The technique seemed to be to hold your breath and look anywhere except in the bucket, while tipping it in the hole and hoping not to get splashed.

Up a flight of iron stairs was the second floor gallery of cells. These cells were occupied by Japanese prisoners. Security seemed to be tighter with the Japs. The guard opened each door individually and the prisoner brought out his own *benki* and put it on the floor.

144

He then went back to his cell and was locked in before we were allowed to pick up the *benki* and put it on the tray. When the tray was full it had to be taken down the stairs to be emptied. It had to be kept level, otherwise all the *benkis* would fall off or the contents would slop about. So, the two men at the back would bend as low as possible, while the two men at the front would lift the loaded tray shoulder high. After each batch of *benkis* was emptied they were hosed down and returned to the cells. There were no toilet facilities as such in the prison. Upstairs there were two offices and even they had *benkis* in them. It was our job to empty them along with those used by the prisoners. The upstairs ones were special and got VIP treatment – a splash of disinfectant.

Finally, we had to hose down the tray, the sump and the yard.

Lined up against a wall in the sun were seven galvanized iron buckets of water, each with a cloth. On an order from the guard we stood in line, each beside a bucket, took off our clothes and tipped the water over ourselves. The water had been standing in the sun for as long as we had been working and had got beautifully warm; what luxury! We dried off on our scrap of towel, got dressed and were escorted back to our cells. I was absolutely exhausted and was glad to sit down on the concrete floor and relax.

Shortly after that, I heard the shuffle of the guard's footsteps. He looked through the slot in the door and said my number, *Di roku aka ju*, to which I automatically said, '*Hai*.' I then heard a whispered conversation and a bowl about the size of a cereal dish appeared on my shelf. When I inspected the dish, it was quite full of rice, vegetables and small pieces of meat, probably pork or chicken. This was the reward for my work. I barely had time to eat it before the guard was back again for the empty dish. If I could manage to do the job, I would get three meals a day instead of two. I spent many anxious hours wondering if I had acquitted myself well enough to get the job. The next morning the guard let me out of my cell and I joined the team again. It seemed that once we got out of the prison buildings the guard relaxed a little and we were allowed to talk very quietly.

It was explained to me that each day we would take it in turns to do a different job. The men who carried the *benkis* from the cells the previous day would carry the tray today. The men who were at the front would be at the back of the tray, which meant I and another

145

man would be at the front. I realized immediately that they were trying me out to see if I could lift the tray shoulder high while going downstairs with a full load. Even today, I can remember that every bone and muscle in my body ached, but I gritted my teeth and got through. On the third morning, I knew I had won my place as a 'poo' carrier when the guard called my number and I stepped out of my cell to become the sixth member of the *benki*-boys' team.

Chapter 22

A Working Prisoner

The morning I became an official *benki*-boy ended in the normal way with a bucket shower and a midday meal. I was spending a great deal of time in solitary confinement and was fantasizing and hallucinating quite frequently. I was 'away with the fairies' when I became aware of some Japs talking quietly near my cell. It is very difficult to put into words the importance that the most minor thing can take on when one is alone. Just a small spider running around the cell becomes something of great interest. The occasional moan of a sick prisoner or the quiet shushing of the guard's feet as he approached my cell, were the only things that broke the silence.

When I heard the Japanese talking I was all ears. My cell door was unlocked and my number was called, *'Di roku aka ju'*. The guards motioned me to step out into the hall and I was then taken to a cell about three or four doors along. One of the guards called out a number and I heard the answer, *'Hai'*. The cell door was opened and I was told to go in. I stepped inside and the door was locked behind me.

My cellmate was one of the *benki* men. Although I had been seeing him for three days, he was just another person doing the job. I didn't know his name as the Japs always called us by our numbers. Meeting him face to face was very different to working with him. I remember him as being taller than me and although he was lean he looked fit. Against him I felt a skinny undersized runt, which I suppose I was. I felt quite nervous and intimidated at first, which was quite natural after being alone for so long.

Of course, normal conversation was impossible as strict silence was imposed by the Japs. We introduced ourselves by means of whispered information, interrupted by numerous visits from the guard. I had taken the place of Jeff's previous cellmate, who had served his time and had been returned to Changi POW camp. The

Japs had put all of our working party into adjacent cells, not because they thought we would enjoy each other's company, but because it was easier to open three cells close to one another, and they were getting short of cells anyway.

My cellmate was an Australian. Soon we had learnt something of each other's history. He, like me, had escaped but had been befriended by a Chinese family who had looked after him, which was why he looked so fit. Word had reached the village where he was hiding that the Japanese were looking for him. Rather than get the Chinese family into trouble Jeff had gone off into the jungle to be captured. Jeff was in no doubt that had he been captured whilst he was with them they would have been killed. He, too, had a long sentence to serve.

He was a tall man but had a very gentle nature. His surname was that of a well-known English poet, Shelley, and he said that he was a distant relation of that person and liked to think that he had inherited some of his poetic talent. His favourite poet was, of course, the great Australian Banjo Paterson. He spent hours teaching me poems such as 'The Man from Snowy River' and others, which today I have forgotten but still enjoy hearing.

I, in turn, would quote poems that I had learned at school and doing these things kept our minds alert. Jeff confessed that his last cellmate had come from somewhere near Liverpool and he had spoken only of the women he had taken advantage of and the ramifications of English football. Of course, we talked of many other things such as home and jobs. Writing this it sounds as though we just jabbered away for hours. The fact was that it was quite difficult to converse even in whispers.

On many occasions we heard a cell door being unlocked and a person was taken out into the yard. We would then hear the distant sound of blows and cries of pain. Later, we would hear a cell door closing and then the moans of someone who had been beaten up for some small misdemeanour. Neither Jeff nor I wanted to join the company of those who had been beaten up so our conversation was very limited.

Each day we did our job and each day I began to feel a little stronger. I am not sure how long Jeff and I were on the job, nor can I remember the names of any of the other members of the team, that is, if I ever got to know them. At a guess I would estimate it was about three months.

One morning we finished our rounds and undressed for our bucket shower, when our clothes were taken away. This was a new development. We dried ourselves and stood about naked for about fifteen minutes. I had a horrible feeling that something was wrong as I could see that the other four members of the team were looking most uncomfortable standing there naked. Eventually, two guards came into the yard with an officer. One guard threw our clothes on the ground and signalled us to get dressed. We were then marched into the prison and made to stand in front of our cell doors. Suddenly the officer let go a torrent of Japanese, directed at us. Of course, we couldn't understand a word of what he was saying. As he was speaking he came to each of us and in his hand he was holding two pencil stubs. A guard who was following was showing us some squares of white Jeyes toilet paper with writing on them. Fortunately, neither Jeff nor I were implicated directly, but we were punished with the others.

Unbeknown to Jeff and I, when we were doing the offices one of the men had seen a stub of pencil on the desk and had picked it up and managed to hide it in his clothing. He had then hidden it in his cell. He had managed to acquire a couple of sheets of paper to write on. Had it stopped at that things wouldn't have been so bad but the other two members of the party had done the same thing and had been writing notes to each other and passing them on whilst on the work party. I don't know whether the Japs had missed the pencil stubs or had found out what was going on, but they searched our cells and found both the paper and the pencils. Even though nothing was found in our cell we lost the job and the extra ration of food. We were given one hour a day of hard physical exercise to the sound of *ichi, ni, san, shi, go, roku, shichi, hachi*. I think the worst punishment of all was when we found a band of Indians had been given our job and we would see their triumphant grinning faces every day.

During my time emptying *benkis* I had seen the other members of my escape party but was barely able to whisper a word or two to them. They all looked in a pretty bad way. One man, known to us as 'Charlie', was constantly calling out and we could see that he was mentally unbalanced. We could often hear the Japs shouting at him and slapping him to make him be quiet.

Not too long after we lost our jobs Jeff became ill – vomiting and diarrhoea were the first symptoms. Soon Jeff became so ill that he couldn't even eat the smallest quantity of the terrible food we were given. I knew that to get any help we had to return Jeff's food uneaten to the guards. I had already returned his partially eaten food bowls to the Indians who served it with no results. I still believe to this day that they ate any food that was left by the other sick prisoners. It took a great effort on my part not to eat some of the food that Jeff couldn't eat.

On the third day Jeff had had a particularly bad night before and was very sick. The cell was in a mess. The guard came to let me out and I managed to get him to come into the cell and see what a mess Jeff was in. On seeing the state of the cell he called another guard and spoke to him. I heard the words, 'laxan bioky,' which I knew meant, 'Very sick'. The guard disappeared and I was taken out for my wash and ten minutes exercise. When I got back the guards were with Jeff, as was a man with a medical armband. Fortunately, he spoke enough English and I enough Japanese to make him understand that Jeff had been ill for about three days. I tried to tell him the Indians had ignored my pleas for help.

Once I had explained this I was put into another cell. There seemed to be a lot of activity going on which, of course, I couldn't see, and finally, the sounds of the cell being washed out. I was not returned to the cell I had occupied with Jeff. I heard later that Jeff had been taken to Changi Hospital, along with Charlie who apparently was suffering from delusions. The Indians who had failed to report Jeff's illness had been sacked. It appeared that the Japs were not averse to starving us to death, or working us to death, but they did not want us to die in their prison. So, if someone was on the point of death, they sent them out to Changi to die. As for me, I was once again in solitary confinement.

We might be silent in prison but there was noise from the Japs, both the guards and the prisoners. During the morning there was the eternal *ichi, ni, san, shi, go, roku, shichi, hachi* as the Japanese exercised. Not too far away from my cell was a hall with a wooden floor. For a long time I had heard the sound of many feet stamping on the floor. I had also heard the sound of oaths and ayahs and, of course, many Japanese words shouted loudly. At the time I thought, 'My God, they even beat up their own prisoners,' but I found out later that it was the guards practising sword fighting – the skills of Samurai warriors.

To do this the men wear a heavy protective uniform with leather padding on the neck and shoulders. A heavy leather helmet covers the head and has a wire gauze face mask. A wooden pole about the same size and weight of the sword is then used to emulate a stylized method of sword fighting. I had seen this done after the war and I believe stories that Japanese officers could sever a man's head with one blow were true.

These and other noises at least kept one's mind alert even in solitary confinement.

Not too long after Jeff and Charlie left the prison, the British and Australian prisoners were let out of our cells after the morning meal. We were marched to a courtyard where we were made to sit in three rows on the dirt floor. There were about twenty or so of us. Once we were seated one of the guards went to a large wicker basket and began producing some dirty black water bottles that looked as though they had been in a fire. He handed them around and when I received mine I realized that it was indeed a fire-blackened aluminium water bottle. We were then each given a small container with some pumice powder in it, some water and a piece of rag. The Japanese guard then showed us how we were expected to make each dirty bottle gleam and sparkle so that it looked brand new.

As I started cleaning my first bottle and gradually seeing the dirt coming off it I became totally absorbed in what I was doing. It was a very dirty job. My hands were black with dirt and pumice powder. After we finished we rinsed the bottles in a 44gal drum of water. I took my time rinsing my bottles as it gave me a chance to clean my hands. As each bottle was finished it would be inspected by the guard and, if satisfactory, you would be handed another to clean. We worked for about three hours a day and were usually back in our cells before the hottest part of the day. I don't know how we would have coped had we been out in the yard in the really hot sun with no protective headwear. It seemed only a very short time before this bottle cleaning interlude ended and we were all back to the normal prison regime.

Even as a child I had never been very supple and to sit cross-legged even for a short time was uncomfortable. I was beginning to notice that my muscles were stiffening up and was having difficulty moving. Shortly after that I started to become bloated. I knew that I was developing beriberi, a disease caused by lack of vitamins. If left untreated this disease is terminal and I was fully aware of what I was in for. Soon I was so bloated that I could not put my shorts on and I could not do up the buttons on my shirt. Even though the

151

guards could see that I was ill they still insisted that I go out for my morning wash, and *ichi, ni, san, shi, go, roku, shichi, hachi*. The bastards seemed to take a delight in waiting until a prisoner was almost at death's door before doing anything about it. The only thing I could do was to continue not eating my food until either I died of starvation or beriberi, or they let me out to Changi Hospital.

Finally, the guards left me alone in my cell and I just lay there. It was agony to turn over on the concrete floor – my skin was tight as my body swelled. I felt as though my whole being was on fire. I was fading in and out of consciousness and was hardly aware of anything that was going on. I had resigned myself to ending my life in the cell.

One day I heard the cell door open and felt hands lifting me up. The pain when they lifted me was so great that I remember screaming out. I was carried out into the daylight and even that hurt my eyes. I was then lifted on to a conveyance of some sort. A motor started up and I remember nothing else until I woke up in a real bed with clean white sheets covering me. Frankly, I thought I had died, but I was in Changi Hospital.

Chapter 23

Return to Changi

People from Outram Road Prison had special priority, not because the Japs had any sympathy for us but because they wanted us back to finish our sentences. Of course, I was not aware of this fact but it did mean that the hospital staff were actually trying to save my life.

I remember drifting in and out of consciousness and someone injecting me in the arm. At last I became aware of things around me and of the fact that I really was alive and in hospital. I was first fed a liquid diet, mainly Marmite soup, and a watered down soya bean sauce, both of which are rich in vitamin B. I then graduated to vegetable soup. I wanted to urinate and I called for a bed bottle. That bottle was my constant companion for about three days. I must have peed gallons of water. The swelling of my body rapidly went down and I began to feel alive again.

During this time someone came and stood at the bottom of my bed and asked my Army number. I told him 5830401 and he asked me if I was Corporal Peter Jackson, to which I replied that I was. With that he said, 'Well, you'd better have these,' and threw a small bundle of letters on my bed. I had left England over two-and-a-half years earlier. These were the first letters I had received since embarking on the troopship; that alone gave me the urge to live. The letters were from my wife, Margaret, and my parents. It took me quite a while to read them in between sleeping and peeing.

At first I didn't recognize the man treating me as a doctor. He looked just like all us other prisoners. He was obviously trying to retain some sense of respectability. His clothes, although threadbare, were scrupulously clean and his beard and hair were neatly trimmed. But he was so thin and haggard that he looked barely able to walk. I have mentioned the word 'hospital' several times previously, but it was more of a sick bay and the medical treatment was of the most basic kind. The Japs kept most of the medical supplies for their own people.

As the days passed I began to take more interest in what was going on. The men in the ward were mainly Australian. There were two from Sumatra and I was the only Englishman. They began to ask questions about where I was from and which regiment I belonged to. I told them that I had made an escape bid in Thailand and had been a prisoner in Outram Road. I asked if anyone knew of Jeff and one of the Australians who had been in the sick bay for a long time told me that Jeff had died only two days after arriving at Changi. He had suffered a massive attack of dysentery and the doctors had not been able to save his life. During the time that I had been a prisoner I had become very hard and callous, almost insensitive to what was going on around me., But at the news of Jeff's death I found that I really cared about him and became very upset.

The man who told me about Jeff was named Steve. I explained to him how I had shared a cell with Jeff in the prison and had grown to like him. Later in the day I saw Steve talking to the doctor. From the way they kept looking over my way I gathered they were talking about me. A little while later the doctor came over and handed me a postcard of the Australian ship *Wanganella*. He explained that when Jeff had been brought from the prison the Japanese had also brought his small packet of belongings. When Jeff had died the doctor had taken charge of Jeff's personal things. The postcard had no address on it but written on the back of the card was a message from Jeff's sister. The doctor thought that as Jeff and I had been friends it would be nice for me to have the postcard as a keepsake. I gratefully accepted the offer and as it turned out, Jeff had done me a favour.

I spoke to the other men but not at any great length. It appeared that all of us had committed some misdemeanour that led to imprisonment or punishment. Steve had been beaten up for talking to a Singaporean whilst on a working party. The Japanese had broken his arm in two places and it had never healed properly.

There were two hospital orderlies (nurses) and one came to me and said that I was now due to go on to ordinary rations. I had lost nearly all my bloatedness but they had been giving me emergency treatment. I would be going back to only having two meals per day. The evening meal consisted of a small ladle of plain boiled rice with a little salt added, and a fried flavoured rissole about the size of a scone. Breakfast the next morning was the same. Needless to say, after the first day I was feeling hungry. Also, I had become accustomed to the taste of the soy sauce on the rice but that had gone.

I had noticed that when the food came to the ward a few people seemed to be doing something to it before they ate. The mystery was explained when I heard the sound of a bottle falling over and I saw one of the men pick up a bottle of soy sauce. I asked Steve how the man had got it and he surprised me by saying that he had bought it. I asked Steve what with and he answered, 'With money, of course.' Apparently one of the hospital orderlies had a contact outside the camp who would buy anything of value from prisoners or exchange it for goods.

I thought long and hard about what he had said and decided that I would have to sell my most treasured possession – the gold ring my Scottish lass had given me. When I was taken from the prison to Changi someone had thought to throw my haversack on me and I had it down by the side of my bed.

Not long after the fall of Singapore all of us troops had realized what a thieving lot the Japs were and had tried, if it were possible, to hide any valuables we owned. My only valuable was the ring. To hide it I had cut the stitching where the shoulder strap on my pack joined the bag itself. I had worked the ring into the shoulder strap and sewed it up again. By doing that I had hoped to keep it until I returned to England.

I decided that if I was going on another starvation diet, at least it would be a tasty one. Also, if I was going to die I would have had the benefit of any money I got for my ring. On the pretext of wanting to cut my fingernails I asked one of the orderlies if he could lend me a pair of scissors. He flatly refused, saying they were for surgical use only, but he was able to lend me a nail file. Whilst I was filing my nails I surreptitiously managed to break the stitches on my pack. Once night-time came I worked my ring out of the shoulder strap and put it on my finger. Actually, I had grown so thin that it was difficult to decide which finger to put it on.

I suppose the best way to describe Steve was as a sort of 'middle man'. He always seemed to know someone who could do something, or sell or buy something, but would never tell you who it was that he was doing the business with. I showed him the ring and he said he would see what he could do about it. He had no idea of its value, but then neither had I. I was more or less working on the

155

theory that if I was going to be swindled I wouldn't make it too easy to be 'done over'.

The Japs had floated their own currency in Singapore but it was practically worthless and no-one wanted to use it. There was still some Singaporean currency around but it was not in general use except on the black market. The first offer I got was forty Singaporean dollars. I was wise enough not to accept the offer and finally got fifty dollars and a bottle of 'wog' sauce. This was the first time that I had had any money in my hand since the week we were captured. Any money that I had been captured with had been spent on buying food from the natives when that was possible. I have no doubt that the ring was worth more and that Steve got a bonus from the sale but I couldn't have sold it myself without his help. Steve mentioned that he could get odd tins of food such as tinned fish, condensed milk, even corned beef, cocoa or Milo. I was loath to spend my money on such luxuries, tempting as they sounded. I knew that at the prices Steve charged, my money would be gone in a week.

I must have become accustomed to eating very little as I found that when I used the 'wog' sauce on my food it helped to satisfy my hunger. I had been in hospital for about a week and the swelling from my beriberi had almost disappeared, but I was painfully thin.

By this time I was able to walk around and chat to some of the other men. On two occasions I had walked out of the ward and into the main building but each time one of the orderlies had sent me back into the ward.

I got up one morning to wash and shave (I had been given a small piece of soap and a safety razor) when one of the orderlies came into the washroom and said, 'Quick, get back into bed and look as though you're dying.'

Of course, I said, 'What's up?'

His answer was: 'Don't argue, do as I say and hurry up.' I left my gear in the washroom, got back into bed and pretended to be asleep. A few moments later I heard a voice say something in Japanese and then I heard, '*Di roku aka ju*,' and my name. I thought, 'My God, the Japs have come to take me back to the prison.' I heard the Japs and the doctor approach my bed and the doctor said, 'Wake up Jackson, you have a visitor.' I looked up to see a Japanese officer peering down at me. I can't describe how I felt. I know I wasn't frightened and all I could think of was that I had to pretend I was really ill.

156

The man ordered the doctor to uncover me, which he did. They then had a discussion (the doctor spoke some Japanese). The Jap then started to feel my body, my arms, legs, stomach and then ordered me to turn over on to my stomach. After that the doctor helped me to sit up and the Jap borrowed his stethoscope, sounding my back and chest. While he was poking me about I tried to imagine what I would be like if I really was dying. When he made me turn on my stomach I groaned and made it seem as though it was a very painful thing to do. Finally, the doctor told me to lie down as they had finished their inspection of me and they both went out of the ward.

Eventually, the doctor returned and told me that between us we had fooled the Japanese into thinking that I was worse than I really was. However, the Japanese officer was adamant that as soon as I was fit enough I was going back to the Outram Road Prison. He had ordered that my food intake should be stepped up to hasten my recovery. The doctor also told me that the Japs paid irregular visits to the ward just to check on the patients.

The next morning I received my usual small breakfast and I thought that's good, nothing extra, because I had been awake most of the night worrying about getting fat and going back to the prison. Sometime around midday one of the orderlies came into the ward with a tray and on it was a bowl covered by a cloth. He put the tray down at the side of my bed and said, 'You'd better get this down you.' When I uncovered it, it was a bowl of thick green vegetable soup. This was the start of my fattening-up diet. I looked at the thick green mess and tried a spoonful of it. It had a bland indefinable taste. I managed to eat about half of it. Upon his return the orderly said I would have to do better than that.

When the evening meal came I seemed to have an extra portion of rice but I did not put any of my precious soy sauce on it. The next day I was again brought the midday soup, with the same instruction to eat it all up (memories of my school days). This time I did eat it all and within about two hours I was violently sick and lost the lot!

The idea of going back to the prison had worried me so much that I suppose today I would be called an anorexic. Fear of putting on weight had affected me to the extent that my stomach rebelled against everything I ate. The doctor and the orderlies tried all ways to make me eat but whatever I ate just would not stay down. I knew that every day I was getting weaker but I was willing to face death rather than go back to the prison.

The Japanese officer – I'm not sure whether he was a doctor – visited me again and went through the same routine as before. When they had left the room I heard the Japanese talking quite loudly to our doctor. The doctor came back into the ward shortly after he had gone and was furious; not with me, but with the Japs. He said, 'The bastards killed poor Jeff but they're not going to do the same to you. Have you any identification tags?' I told him I had lost mine. He then asked me if I could spare a couple of my letters to identify myself. I sorted out a couple that I thought were the least important ones and, finally, he asked if I was willing to give him my haversack. I didn't seem to have much choice. The doctor took it away and in exchange gave me a small canvas bag to keep my few valuables in.

Later, the doctor told me that he was going to let me out of the ward, not into Changi Prison Camp but to another one outside the walls. He warned me that the food I would get in the camp would be even less than the hospital rations but at least I would be able to eat without fear of going back to Outram Road. Steve said that he would come and see me now and again to check how I was getting on.

Just before dusk a man came and said that I was to go with him. Although I was very weak, I was still able to walk. I followed him out of the ward into a passage with a pair of double doors at the end. When we stepped through the doors I found myself in the main block of Changi Prison. Around me were lots of other prisoners – some lying on the floor on blankets, others in cells with open doors and others just standing around talking. None of them seemed to take the slightest bit of notice of us. I was led through the building and out through a gate in the wall of the prison to an open space, in which there were several palm leaf thatched huts. He took me to one of the huts and in it was the usual raised platform for sleeping on. We walked down the centre gangway and about halfway down he pointed out a vacant space with some blankets and one or two other odds and ends. This was my new home.

Before he left me he told me that what I had thought to be a hospital ward had actually been the old Changi Prison sick bay. The doctor who had been attending to me was an officer in the Royal Army Medical Corp (RAMC). He wished me luck and left me to draw my own conclusions as to how they were going to wangle my disappearance from the sick bay. I must admit that it was a week or two before I felt really safe. Also, I found that my appetite had returned and what had been said about small rations was quite true. It must seem that I spend a lot of time talking about food. Well, I spent most of my time thinking about food. In spite of being economical with my soy sauce it finally ran out and I missed it terribly.

The men with whom I shared my new home, were a mixture of British and Australian soldiers and I soon became friends with them. Unfortunately, we were all suffering the effects of serious malnutrition. I myself was lucky in the fact that I had no return of beriberi but just remained very thin and weak. Some of the other men had been wounded in the fighting and had lost limbs or the use of them. Others had been very ill and had never fully recovered, so we were a sorry looking lot. Incidentally, I heard that Charlie, who had been sent to Changi with Jeff, had gone completely mad and was locked up in solitary confinement where no-one was allowed to see him.

I had been in the hut a few days when I had a visit from Steve. It was primarily a social visit and we had quite a long chat. The subject of money came up and I told him that I still had my fifty dollars tucked safely away. I also told him that I could do with some more soy sauce. He told me that he could still get goods on the black market but couldn't tell me when. If I trusted him he would see what he could do for me. He also asked me if I wanted any tobacco. I told him I did, but not at his prices. He then said to leave it to him as he had a little deal going with regard to tobacco. The upshot of this discussion was that I parted with twenty dollars. A couple of days passed and I was beginning to wonder about it when Steve turned up with a small cardboard box. In the box was a bottle of sauce, a tin of herrings in tomato sauce, and wrapped in paper was what looked like a lot of brown dead flower stalks.

I was very pleased with the sauce and tin of fish but not with the brown stalks. I asked him what the stalks were and he said, 'Smell them.' When I smelt them they had a very strong smell of tobacco, which is what they were – tobacco stalks. I still wanted to know what use they were to me. He explained that they were not for me personally but he wanted me to work on them for him and he would cut me in on any money he made from them. Later that day he returned with a metal dish hidden under a small tattered towel. From each pocket he produced two small jars; one contained sugar and the other rum. He explained that they were to treat the tobacco stalks.

In the prison camp environment we had no privacy whatsoever and so all our business was carried on in whispered conversations. We all had to trust one another and only on rare occasions was anything stolen. All the same, Steve warned me that I was responsible for the goods he had brought me.

The tobacco stalks were from the top of the plants and were quite soft and pliable, containing a fair amount of tobacco flavour. I had to make up a syrup of the sugar and rum, just enough to cover the tobacco stalks, then watch until the stalks had soaked up the liquid. I then waited until they had dried out sufficiently to handle and tie them up tightly in small bundles. When they were nearly dry they stuck together through the action of sugar and rum water. At this stage the bundles were about 1½in in diameter. They smelt very pleasant; in fact, they were almost as good as pipe tobacco. I was getting a bit anxious in case someone did pinch some. Steve visited me a couple of times and guided me through the processing. Once he was satisfied that the bundles had the right moisture content he gave me the final job, which was the most difficult.

I had finished up with three bundles, each about 8in or 9in long. Steve gave me an old knife which was very sharp and I had to cut the bundles up into sections about an inch long so that I finished up with plugs of tobacco 1½in by 1in. It was a messy tedious job but I managed it somehow. I had to put the finished plugs in the dish and cover them with a damp cloth to prevent them from drying out. When Steve came to collect the tobacco he gave me a few pieces of tissue paper about the same size as cigarette papers. He picked out one of the plugs of tobacco and said I should see what I thought of it.

To smoke it you have to get a cloth or some paper and pull the plug to pieces until you have a heap of fine shreds and then roll a smoke in the tissue paper. Once it was pulled to pieces it was surprising how much tobacco there was in one plug. It probably wouldn't pass muster today but I found it a very pleasant smoke. Of course, the smell in the hut couldn't be disguised and so I had to offer some to a couple of my nearest companions.

I don't know how much Steve sold it for, or who to. He asked me if I wanted money or goods for my work. I said that I preferred goods and so I had several different tins of food delivered. A tin of corned beef was a prize and not something to be scoffed in one go. I made it last for three or four meals by mixing it with rice rations. This made it more tasty and possibly more nourishing.

I did another two batches of tobacco for Steve, plus one other tedious job making cigarette papers. After all, it's not much good selling tobacco without the papers to roll it in. Steve taught me how the tissue paper was made. First you needed some good quality paper, usually found in art books or technical manuals or, better still, from old bibles. Take a leaf from the book and carefully cut diagonally across the corner of the page about half-an-inch in and not right through the paper. Fold the corner over and, if the paper is the right texture, it is possible to carefully peel the page apart and finish up with two pieces of tissue-thin paper. This does require a lot of patience, but in a prison camp one has time. Finally you cut the paper into cigarette paper-sized pieces and make them up into bundles of a convenient number to sell or trade.

Paper of any kind was a valuable commodity; even newspaper was treasured, not for its reading value as most of it was written in Japanese, but for other purposes. Steve had given me a pencil to write down the numbers of papers I had done. In the book he had given me to cannibalize I found two or three sheets of unprinted paper which I kept for my own use.

I have always been fond of drawing and one afternoon I got out the postcard of the *Wanganella* and decided to draw a slightly larger copy of it. A couple of other inmates wanted to know what I was drawing. I must have made a fair copy of it as my mates were quite impressed. One of them was an Australian and wanted to show it around to his friends. The *Wanganella* was as well-known to the Australians as the *Queen Mary* was to us Brits. In peacetime it did the trans-Tasman journey and during the war became a hospital ship.

My drawings of the ship were popular as I sold, swapped or traded several of them for small articles. I swapped one drawing of the huts for an Indonesian bible. None of us could read it so I had no hesitation in cutting it up for cigarette paper. Steve was always ready to take any cigarette papers off me as he had a ready sale for most things produced in the camp.

Perhaps I have made all these things sound too easy. Anything we did had to be done with great caution as the Japanese often came

161

through and either destroyed or requisitioned anything that displeased them. This applied, particularly, to drawings of the camp. However, by taking the risk of doing the few odd jobs I have mentioned, it helped me get a few extras that I needed. Also I was able to hold onto the small amount of money that I had got for the sale of my ring. I suppose, indirectly, wee Scots Margaret had helped to at least make things a little better for me in the prison camp. She may even have saved my life.

One of the men I had become friendly with was a churchgoer and he had encouraged me to go with him. There was no actual church as such but each denomination had made an attempt to build some place of worship. They ranged from a screened area with sackcloth to a purpose-built hut complete with altar. The church I attended was Church of England and consisted of an open-fronted thatched hut. There was an altar and a crucifix, and some wooden candle holders with artificial candles. It was all quite tastefully done. I was quite impressed and told the padre how much I admired it, saying that I would like to do a drawing of it.

I drew the church on the lid of a white box that Steve had given me. The padre asked me if he could have it. Of course I couldn't refuse and so handed it over. I did another one for myself but somehow it wasn't as good as the first one and I was rather disappointed with it.

I had been out of Outram Road for about five months and had more or less forgotten about it. I hadn't seen Steve for quite some time and took it for granted that he had other fish to fry, until one afternoon he came to the hut and said, 'Don't argue, just grab all your gear and come with me.' I knew by the urgency in his voice that something serious was going on. He took me into Changi grounds, leaving me with a group of his friends who lived in the buildings and telling me to stay with them. Someone, probably an officer, had got a secret radio and the Japs had heard of it. They were going through the camp with a fine-toothed comb, questioning everyone and searching all their belongings. There was always some person who thought he was doing an heroic deed by using a secret radio. But it was a stupid thing to do because it not only jeopardized their own safety, or even their life, but affected all those in the camp.

The Japs systematically searched each hut, destroying belongings and, in many cases, beating men to try and make them tell where the radio was hidden. If the radio was found, the man who operated it

162

was punished, usually very severely. The trouble was though that a lot of innocent people were made to suffer unnecessarily before the offender was caught. On the other hand, if the Japs did not find the radio, it was not unknown for a whole camp to be put on even shorter rations than the usual meagre allowance. In many cases, men were tortured if the Japs suspected them of knowing anything about it.

No-one wanted me to get tangled up in a radio search. I was a prisoner from Outram Road gaol and should have been returned there when I was well again. Had the Japs discovered who I was, there would have been bad consequences for many people. As it happened, the Japs had apparently given up the search before they got to the hut where I had been living. Whether they found the radio or not I never found out; I doubt if one even existed. However, it was best to stay with my friends in Changi Prison until the heat was off.

After this episode I thought it prudent not to do any more drawings or participate in any activities that would draw attention to myself. This meant that there was no way I could earn anything, either in the way of goods or money, so I was on the verge of starvation. What little I had been able to buy before had only been enough to tickle my taste buds. The days drifted by and I lost all sense of time; days and nights came and went.

The area I now lived in was supposed to be a hospital camp. This was in name only as there was no medical treatment and if men got too ill they just died. The only advantage it had was that the Japanese had written us off as too sick to be bothered about. The disadvantage was that our rations were even smaller than in Changi Prison.

Even though I was quite weak I was still able to walk about. On odd occasions I was able to visit my friends in Changi. There I heard that the Japs were even more aggressive than usual and the rations had been getting smaller. They had made threats on more than one occasion that if the worst happened they would be quite capable of annihilating all of us. There had been an undercurrent among the POWs that if it ever came to that, we would revolt and at least we would be able to say, 'One of you for one of us.'

One day in the early hours of the morning I heard several distinct thumps in the distance. Actually, I think I felt rather than heard them. I asked my nearest bed mate if he had heard or felt anything and he said he had. As the days passed the whole camp became aware that something was going on. We heard the noise of aircraft and what were obviously the sounds of warfare. Whose planes and guns or what bombs were falling, we didn't know.

One day our prayers and our questions were answered. A large plane flew over and suddenly the sky became white with paper as hundreds of leaflets came down. When we read them the whole camp became a place of great joy. We hugged each other, and we were laughing and crying at the same time. We, the living skeletons, were literally dancing with joy. The leaflets told us that the war was over. The Japanese had capitulated and whereas up to this moment they had been our captors, they were now our guardians and held responsible for our welfare. The next day one man, a British officer, walked into the camp and as he passed through he told us that help was on its way.

Chapter 24

Freedom

Within a few days of the lone officer's visit the very sick men were being given urgent medical treatment. The rest of us who were malnourished but otherwise reasonably fit, were issued with some decent clothing. Food began to flow into the camp. We were warned by the 'powers that be' to be careful with our food intake and try not to overeat as we could quite easily overload our stomachs. Most of us heeded the warning but there were those who did not and suffered illness and, in some cases, even death.

I heard that my friends who had escaped with me from the railway camp in Thailand (Siam) had been released from Outram Road Prison. I also heard that Ian's younger brother, Bernard, had died. Unfortunately, I did not see them again.

I suppose each one of us had a great experience. The greatest moment for me, as for most others, was when someone came and asked my name and number and whether I wished to send a telegram to tell my people I was alive and well. Whoever was responsible for those telegrams did a fantastic job. I was in constant touch with my family for days after our release.

Within a few days some of us were taken out of the camp and put into chalet type buildings. We actually had clean beds and bed linen to sleep on. The chalets were like a small one-bedroom apartment and were shared by two men. We were fed and watered by our own people. I had hoped that I would have one of the Japs to look after me so that I could kick his behind now and again, but no such luck. Before we moved into our new quarters we, and our belongings, had to be deloused and debugged. The whole camp had been louse and bug ridden. If one had needed to get up in the night, it had been possible to see a trail of squashed bugs where one had walked on the wooden boards. It was bad enough having to put up with being bitten by the horrible pests but even worse that they could carry diseases from man to man.

Shortly after being released I was medically examined and assessed as to whether I needed hospital treatment. Fortunately I did not but, as a matter of interest, my weight was 6st 8lb (43kg).

Soon we were paid out some money and those of us who were able were allowed to walk to nearby Changi village to buy bits and pieces, but definitely no food. I was able to walk to the village and it was a great thrill to look in the small shops. Although there was not a great deal to see, I could actually buy something with my money. One shop had some small china models of Chinese pagodas and dragons, as well as Malayan houses on stilts. I thought what lovely little souvenirs they would make. As I was admiring them the lady in the shop said, 'You like?' I said, 'Yes, they are lovely.' She then said for me to wait as she had some special ones to show me. She disappeared for a few minutes and when she returned she had a wooden tray with about a dozen larger and far better looking model houses on it. I was afraid that they were too expensive for me to buy. She then asked me what sort of money I had and I told her Malayan dollars. I selected about six nice pieces and held out my money. She took some and, in farewell, asked me to tell my friends that she had, 'Plenty nice things for English soldiers, good price, no steal money from them.' I did show the things to my friends and I am sure she did quite a good trade from my recommendation.

Another great pleasure was being able to buy English cigarettes again. Although it was almost impossible to buy tobacco during our incarceration I don't think that any of us who had smoked in the past had given any thought to giving up smoking altogether. I know my few puffs of a Wills' 'Goldflake' were like a taste of heaven.

We were all relatively free to wander about and as I got stronger I went exploring the outskirts of the village. One day I came across an empty building that looked interesting and when I pushed the door, it opened quite easily. Inside it looked as though it had been a storehouse of some kind. At the far end of the building were some offices. Just for something to do I decided to investigate further. Inside the offices the desks had been badly treated, and broken chairs lay about. In a row of cupboards along a wall I found lots of paper with both English and Japanese typing on them. The cupboards were about 8in or 9in off the ground and as I looked in one of them I felt my foot touch something underneath the cupboard. I pulled out a cardboard box, which felt quite heavy. It held an almost brand new portable Olympia typewriter. My mind raced around in circles; should I take it or leave it? Then I thought, 'If I don't pinch it, some-one else will,' so I took it out of the box, casually picked it up by the handle and walked back to my billet. I put it under my bed and after tea I couldn't help but get it out and admire it. Two or three minutes later my room-mate came in and saw me fiddling with it. He asked where I had got it and I told him I had bought it. His only comment was, 'You were a lucky bugger.' That's exactly what I thought too.

I practised on the typewriter daily with one finger of each hand but got fed up with only typing about one word a minute. I decided that I would put it away and wait until I got home to have some lessons.

I gradually got stronger and put on some weight. I had made friends with another soldier who had lost a foot in the battle. Although he had been disabled he could get around with a home-made crutch. Like a lot of us, he had decided to stay in Singapore, hoping to be repatriated straight back to England. We went around Changi together and Jack got a lot of sympathy from the local people.

Jack and I were out one afternoon when we met two sailors who were from the battleship HMS *Nelson*. They told us that they had decided to get a taxi and have a tour around Singapore Island. When they had got to Changi they wanted a look around. Rather than keep the taxi waiting they had paid it off. Jack and I spent some time with them, showing them what little there was to see. They asked us if we would like to go back to the ship with them and have a look around it, as they were allowed to have visitors if they wished. Jack and I accepted their invitation gratefully and in no time were in a taxi and on our way to Singapore City.

The ship was anchored off-shore and to get to it we had to nego-tiate entering and exiting a liberty boat that took us from shore to ship. Jack was much admired for the way he managed to nimbly hop around, getting in and out of the boat. The two sailors showed us as much of the ship as they were allowed. When the other sailors saw Jack hopping around with his broomstick crutch on our way around the decks, they seemed to look on him with admiration. Actually, I felt quite jealous of him.

167

After showing us around the ship we were invited to go below to the mess desk. After being introduced all round we finished up having a meal with the sailors. Later, we were put into a taxi and sent back to Changi. I still have a postcard of HMS *Nelson* with the signatures of several men who were on the mess deck at the time.

I was beginning to find that my weight was gaining faster than my strength and it was getting harder for me to get around. When I was lying down it was quite a struggle to get up. However, I was loath to report sick, as it might have delayed my return to England. I heard that a number of the very sick had been, or were going to be, sent to Australia or Ceylon (Sri Lanka). Later, when I met up with a couple of men who had gone to Australia to recuperate, I wished I had taken the opportunity to go as they told me that they had had a wonderful time.

I would have dearly loved to see some of the sights of Singapore but it was not to be. We were suddenly told that we would be embarking on a troopship to go home to England. It was marvellous news, and so it was a quick whisk through Singapore and onto the ship.

Whilst I had been recuperating in Singapore I had been paid. Since there had been very little opportunity to spend money, I had saved quite an amount. Once we had put to sea we found that the canteen was well-stocked with all kinds of cigarettes, tobacco, chocolate, sweets and even cigars, all at duty-free prices. Although it was a British ship, a lot of the goods sold in the canteen were of American origin. Many of us were buying as much as we could to stock up for when we arrived home.

The food on the ship was, to us, first class. As good as the food was, I was not able to eat a great deal. Also, I was still gaining weight so that I was having difficulty in getting up when I had been seated. Getting up from my bunk bed in the morning was a great effort.

I reported sick and the ship's doctor confirmed what I had suspected – I was suffering a recurrence of beriberi. The doctor treated me with injections and drugs without much success. However, I managed to enjoy the trip and the adventure of going through the Suez Canal.

The ship stopped for a short time at Port Said and although we were not allowed to disembark and the port traders were not allowed on the ship, a lot of trading was done by hauling up baskets on ropes. Fortunately, we had a few old soldiers on board and, of course, the crew members. They warned us to unwrap anything that the Egyptians sold. The traders were very adept at selling something that appeared very good on the outside but was rubbish on the inside.

One of the traders had been waving some rather nice looking leather wallets. I was on the lower deck of the ship and could almost reach out and grab the article. I made him understand that I wanted to see it and he held the basket on a pole. He passed up the wallet and I found that it was a writing case of finely tooled leather with a picture of the pyramids and camels on the front. Inside it was lined with sand coloured fabric and was very nicely finished. I ask him how much and we began the usual haggling. Finally, we agreed on the price. Fortunately, I still had the case in my hands when he started demonstrating that I should give him back his sample and he would send me up one wrapped in cellophane. I said, 'No, I want this one.' After quite a lot of gesticulating and obvious bad temper he finally gave in and let me keep the one I had.

A chap who was standing next to me was admiring the case and called out to the trader to send one up for him to look at. Up came one wrapped in cellophane that looked exactly like mine and was the same price. One of the crew members asked if he could have a look at it. The crewman took the packet in his hand and leaning over the rail of the ship started to undo the wrapper. The trader was nearly having a fit – shouting, pointing his finger and stamping his feet. The crewman quietly remarked, 'He's putting a curse on me.' When the wrapper came off he showed us the inside of the case and it was just plain cardboard: no pockets, no fabric, no stitching, just ordinary cardboard. With that the crew member just threw the packet onto the dockside and told the trader to, 'F*** off.'

I was very pleased with my purchase and my companion was pleased he hadn't been done. I remarked about the Egyptian cursing the crew member and he said, 'Oh, don't worry about that, I've cursed him back. The "Gypos" don't like being told to f***-off.' In spite of the warnings that the men had received, a lot of them did get done. Half-empty boxes of exotic looking candy and sweets were very common.

Before we arrived in England the rehab people questioned us as to our final destinations so that when we got off the ship we could be grouped for ongoing transport. Right up until the last minute no-one had told us where we were due to dock. I had been looking for the white cliffs of Dover but instead we arrived at Liverpool docks.

The voyage home to England is easily described by one word – boring. The weather was perfect, the sea calm, and even the odd flying fish landing on deck was cause for excitement. Maybe it is worth mentioning that some of the time I played around with my typewriter, much to the amusement of my fellow travellers. I managed to type very slowly and laboriously a few pages on my experiences in the jungle. On board the ship were officers who were in charge of repatriation and one of their duties was to interview ex-POWs with regard to our treatment by the Japs. One of the officers happened to see what I was doing and was quite complimentary about my efforts. He asked if he could read it when I had finished. He asked if he could keep it for the time being, with a promise that I would get it back. That was fifty years ago; I have never had it back.

Once we were through the Mediterranean and in the Atlantic Ocean the weather began to get a little colder but the sea remained reasonably calm. It was totally different to our trip across the Atlantic to Nova Scotia four years earlier almost to the day. By the time the ship arrived in England we were all very glad to be wearing our serge battledress uniforms.

Chapter 25

The Homecoming

As we steamed into the port the captain gave a warning not to crowd the rail on the shore side as this could upset the balance of the ship. We were excited to at last reach home and the deck was crowded with soldiers. But we did try to get the Liverpudlians to the front so that they could greet their friends and families. On the wharf was a large crowd of people all cheering and waving, shouting out names that we could hardly hear. Men would wave back as they recognized the person calling them.

Everywhere people were holding up signs of welcome with the name of their family member. The order came for all the local men to disembark first. I went below to pack my possessions. They now consisted of a large kitbag stuffed with chocolate, cigarettes, cigars and other odds and ends, including an army blanket I had been given in Singapore. That was rolled up and stuffed in the bottom of my kitbag and there was no way I was going to part with it. There was also my backpack with clothing in it and, of course, my typewriter. I realized that I was going to have to get that lot all the way to London without any help as all the other men were in the same situation.

At last the call came for us to disembark and somehow I managed to stagger down the gangway with my gear. We formed up in our respective groups and soon we were on our way to the train, which was going to take us to London. We all crowded on. Soon, amidst all the excitement, we were on our way home. Those of us that couldn't find a seat were quite content to sit on the floor or on our gear or, if fit enough, to stand and look out of the window. The train driver must have caught our happy feeling as I remember the train whistle blowing at every opportunity.

I knew when we were approaching London as I saw familiar names and places. The train gradually became slower and slower as we approached Euston Station. As it rounded the final bend we heard the roar of the crowd. There were hundreds cheering, the train's whistle was blowing and there was even a band to greet us. All the carriage doors flew open when the train stopped and out we tumbled, dragging our belongings onto the platform. Our arrival at Euston Station was more or less a repeat of the ship's arrival at Liverpool dock. But it was far more emotional as I was now looking for my family.

It looked as if the whole population of London had turned out to greet us. There was a sea of people and everywhere homemade signs were held up with family names on them. I looked to see if my name was among them but couldn't see it and so, picking up my gear, I started to walk up the platform. I had only gone a short distance when I heard a voice calling, 'Peter! Peter!' In the crowd I saw a woman frantically waving to me. It was my wife but the crowd was so dense that she was having difficulty getting to me. When people realized what was happening, they made way for her to get through. She rushed towards me and I let everything fall to the ground. Almost four years to the day since I last held her in my arms, I was holding her once again.

Once we had both calmed down and composed ourselves she explained that she had left my father and mother and my son near the exit in case she missed me. I picked up my belongings and we made our way to where my Mum, Dad and son were. My son was now five years old. Now it was their turn to greet me with hugs and tears and kisses. My mother picked up my son and putting him in my arms said, 'Your Daddy's home at last.'

After hugging me for a few moments my son looked at me and said, 'You do look funny in that hat, Daddy.' This was not a surprising remark as the hats we had been issued with were a khaki beret with a pompom on the top. I felt quite daft wearing it, added to the fact that it was probably more off than on as my face was still swollen with beriberi. It was a wonder my family recognized me.

We headed off in a taxi but it was not the journey I had been expecting. Both my wife and my parents had moved house in my absence. When the taxi arrived at the house I could see a sign stretched across the street which read in big letters: 'Welcome Home, Peter.' As we arrived we were surrounded by neighbours. Once inside the house I found the flat was on the first floor. I was

172

fairly accustomed to climbing stairs on the ship but even so I was puffing with the exertion.

Once we had settled ourselves down and had a cup of tea I produced some chocolate for my son. This was a welcome gift as it was still rationed. On giving my Dad some cigarettes I got, 'Cor blimey, I haven't seen that brand for a long time.' I had, of course, bought some souvenirs for my mother and my wife. It was an exciting time.

My Dad, never one to mince words, remarked that considering I was supposed to have been starved, I was far too fat for my own good. I told him that I fully agreed with him and explained that I was not fat from eating too much food but being ill with beriberi. When I explained this they were all very concerned. All the neighbours and friends wanted to meet me and they were quite surprised to see how fat I was. I was soon telling everyone about beriberi.

Not long after I returned home I started to go through the same weight loss process that I had already experienced in the prison camp. I seemed to be in the toilet half the day and my weight dropped to about 8st (approximately 50kg). From then on I started to regain both my health and strength.

I had bought quite a stock of duty free cigarettes and tobacco whilst on the troopship. When people came to visit me I was always quite generous in handing out cigarettes and tobacco. Later I was to find out, to my own detriment, that I had been far too generous. Eventually, I was down to my last few fags and decided that I would buy a couple of packets of Will's 'Gold Flake' or some Players, or some other well-known brand. I wandered around to the local newspaper and tobacconist's and asked for some cigarettes. I was refused them all by a stony-faced shopkeeper. Finally, he said, 'I've got some Tenner's.' Now I had never heard of those but decided to take a couple of packets rather than none at all.

When I got home I showed them to my wife who also smoked and had helped me to use up my little stock. She was disgusted, saying they were awful. After trying one or two I came to the same conclusion. Later I found out they were called 'horse tails' because they tasted as though they were made from what comes from the rear end of a horse. The next time I went to the shop my wife came with me and introduced me to the shopkeeper. I had not realized that the shops always kept the best of everything for regular customers, hence the saying, 'under the counter,' because that's where all the goodies were kept.

173

After having a week's leave I was reinstated as a fully paid member of His Majesty's Forces. I had been given the rank of sergeant in the field of battle but it had not been a War Substantive rank and so I was still a corporal. I was sent to Kneller Hall at Twickenham, which in peacetime had been the Army School of Music. I was there for rehabilitation. I was able to live at home and commute daily to the hall. Fortunately, a midday meal was supplied and this helped our budget.

I decided to continue my old association with woodwork and took a course in cabinet making. I started with the basics and the instructor soon realized that I had been a tradesman prior to the war. When I explained my experience, he said that I could draw any materials I needed from the timber store. As long as I kept him informed of what I was doing, I could go freelance.

My wife had seen a rather nice folding fire screen with wooden panels that she liked, so I decided to make one for her as a surprise. I made the fire screen and as I had been taught the basics of French polishing before the war, I also French polished it. Anything that was made had to be inspected by someone in authority before we were permitted to take it. I finished my project in the morning and had gone to lunch. When I got back to the workroom I found a note on the fire screen asking me to go and see one of the officers. I knocked on the door and was called in to find an officer sitting at his desk. I went through the usual procedure of standing to attention and saluting. He then very kindly told me not to worry about all that business but to sit down. He said that he had seen what a beautiful job I had made of the fire screen. Could I possibly allow him to take it home and show his wife as she did tapestry and had done one in three sections? He had already telephoned her and told her about the screen. I had intended taking it home myself but had not told my wife what I was making and so I agreed to let him take it.

On the following Monday I had started on my next project; a far more prosaic one this time – a wooden clothes-horse. The woodwork instructor came to me and said I was wanted by the officer who had borrowed my fire screen. I went to see him and he told me his wife was delighted with the design and it was just the thing for her tapestries. He then asked me if I was willing either to sell him the one I had just made or to make another for him. He said he would give me time to think about it.

I weighed up the pros and cons. I had not told my wife about the screen and I realised a clothes-horse was an urgent item. Also, I had no idea how long I was going to be at the rehabilitation unit. I came to the conclusion that it was best to sell him the one he already admired. He was happy with his purchase and I was happy with what he paid me.

A couple of weeks passed and I was still busy with woodwork when the instructor told me that the officer wished to see me again. I duly reported to his office and found him in the company of a youngish man called Tom Biddle. Tom and the officer were friends and Mr Biddle had seen the sample of my handiwork and had been impressed. He was connected to T. Crowther and Sons Antique Dealers of North End Road, Fulham. The firm was extremely busy restoring not only antiques but lots of other valuable furniture and they were looking for competent staff. Mr Biddle thought I fitted into that category and had come to offer me a job interview with the firm. I accepted the offer and, on being shown around and meeting other members of the staff, said I was willing to accept a job there.

When I was actually able to start work depended on my health, which fortunately had stabilized, and my demob from the Army. They were quite prepared to accept an arrangement whereby I joined their company after I was demobbed. This occured on 7 July 1946 and I joined T. Crowther and Sons within a few days of that date. After nearly seven years of mostly hardship and misery, which I had never asked for or deserved, I was once again back to living a normal life.

One final thought about the 'generosity' of the Army. I mentioned that I had been reduced to the rank of corporal. It also seemed that after I had been released from the POW camp I had been rather overpaid while in transit. Something like £50 was deducted from the back pay that had accumulated while I was a prisoner of war. All ex-service men were entitled to a gratuity on leaving the services. Owing to the fact that my wife had had several rises in pay, when I got my gratuity it was a little more than £300. The normal payout for someone in my position would have been at least twice that amount. I had been conscripted into the Army at the age of twenty.

When I became a fully paid-up member of society I was amazed at the number of men of my own age who had never served in any of the forces. My best friend had never been called up as his father had an engineering business and had been able to get his son exempted on the basis that he was doing vital war work.

One day I overheard two men talking to each other during a lunch break. They were discussing how much they had been paid for their week's work and how much they would have earned during wartime making ammunition boxes. They had been on night shift as overseers for the women workers. For working one night shift they had been paid a special rate which was almost double what they were now earning. They went on to discuss the other benefits of their job such as, 'Do you remember Betty? Gawd, she was a good 'un. I spent many an hour with her down behind the benches.' The other one had spent a lot of time in the storeroom when some of the women went to get more supplies. They were really bemoaning the fact that the war was over. This took place in a café and both had large cups of tea on the table. I had finished my lunch and I was still in uniform. I got up from my table and as I passed by them I deliberately bumped into their table, causing their cups of tea to slop everywhere. As I went out, I could hear them swearing about it but they didn't come after me as I thought they might have done.

When I saw the damage the German bombing had done to London I was appalled. I realized that the civilian population must have suffered to some degree even more than those of us in the army. My mother told me that my father had spent many nights going out into the streets after a big air-raid, helping the rescue crews to get people out of the debris. Sometimes he would be out nearly all night and would still go to work the next day.

Another thing that shocked me was an exhibition of photographs of Germany. Many of them were the usual photos of the devastation caused by the Allied bombing. Some were of the deliberate destruction of places by the retreating German army. Others showed both Allied and German dead. There was a special part of the exhibition showing the Jewish extermination camps, like Auschwitz. There were piles of skeleton-like corpses and mass graves. Even worse were the terrible looks on the faces of the living skeletons. In all my time in the Far East I had never seen anything like those photographs. At first I could not believe what I was looking at. I had met one or two young German people in peacetime and looked upon them as being similar to the English. It seemed inconceivable that the Germans could do such dreadful things to anyone, whatever their race.

The truth became even worse when it was revealed that the Germans had been not only exterminating the Jews but had treated other races like Poles, Gypsies and Russians with immense cruelty. One unforgettable photo showed a French village square with a memorial in the centre and around it was a pile of dead French civilians. These men had been shot in reprisal for the death of one German soldier who had been killed in an accident with a French driver. When I left that exhibition I hated what men could do to other members of humanity.

However, as I have so often been told, 'Pete, my boy, you're lucky to be alive to tell the tale, so let's forgive and forget.'

Epilogue

No one in the world asks to be born. We have no control over that and, from my own experience, very little control over much else. Fate seems to play a great part in most people's lives. Looking back on mine, if I had done what I wanted to do at certain times, I would probably not be here writing this. When I wanted to go into the army I was refused. When I didn't want to go into the army I was conscripted with no way out. When a lot of my fellow soldiers went overseas I was kept back, and so it went on, fate taking a hand time after time. It has even been said that I was lucky to miss out on 'D-Day'. I couldn't agree more, but I will say that most of the men who were in that dreadful carnage had a good time in England before they went into battle.

I think seventy-five per cent of young men like me had no wish to be in the army, but we had no choice. The whole world was being attacked by a horde of madmen and so, as peace loving as most of us were, we had to try to defend our country, our homes and our loved ones as best we could.

With regard to my own army service in Singapore, I survived. Why? I don't know. Again, fate took a hand. A great many of my Company died in that battle. Some I knew, a good many others I didn't but, nonetheless, they were all comrades. In 1980 I visited Singapore on a holiday and I went to Changi War Cemetery. I walked amongst rows and rows of graves, each one with a name and number on the headstone and the age of the man who was buried there. Nearly all of them were barely out of their teens, nineteen to twenty-four mostly, with the occasional thirty-five to forty-year old who was either an old solider or an officer.

You have read my story. It is more than sixty years since these things happened to me. They have been buried in my memory all this time. Some memories are just brief flashes; others are of really traumatic events. Some things are just not possible to describe unless you live through them. What you have read is not a novel; they are actual events. I have not tried to embroider them just to fill up a few extra pages or to pretend that I did some great heroic action. Other books have been written by people who witnessed Japanese atrocities first-hand. I know they happened but, fortunately, I was spared those experiences.

I never saw the Moulmein Pagoda they sing about in the old song, 'On the Road to Mandalay.' It mentions looking eastward to the sea, but I couldn't see it from my prison cell. However, I can boast that I walked through the jungle in bare feet to the city where it is. I did not go to Bangkok as a wide-eyed tourist, although I did travel from Bangkok to Singapore by train free of charge, even if it was in an old covered railway wagon. I didn't see the Golden Buddha or the Imperial Palace or stay in big flash hotels. Instead I was tried by four or five Japanese officers and sentenced to life imprisonment. I have been fortunate enough to visit Singapore three times since the war and consider it a marvellous island but completely changed from what little I managed to see of it in wartime.

179

Publisher's Notes

The Suffolk Regiment
Peter Jackson joined the Suffolk regiment, stationed in Bury St Edmunds, in 1939. This was one of Britain's more historic regiments having been founded in 1685 and comprised men mainly from Norfolk and Suffolk. It was originally called the 'Duke of Norfolk's Regiment on Foot' (nicknamed the 'Old Dozen'). It remained an infantry division and its men served in the Boer War and in India.

The regiment saw early action in the First World War. On 26 August 1914 the second Battalion undertook a fierce rear-guard action in the defence of Le Cateau. Here they were gradually outflanked during the eight hours of incessant fighting. The Germans knowing they had no hope of survival entreated them to surrender. The German buglers even sounded the British ceasefire in an effort to get them to lay down their arms. Eventually they were rushed from the rear and those that survived were taken into captivity. Of the 1,000 men who fought 720 were killed, wounded or captured.

In 1941 the 4th and 5th Battalions (Territorial Army) were posted first to India and then transferred to Singapore. It is this story that Peter records in his memoir. They arrived as the island was being evacuated and all those who survived became prisoners of the Japanese. Peter was one of the few of those who lived through this ordeal and he is believed to be one of the last of those who were imprisoned still to be alive.

In 1959 the regiment was absorbed into the 1st East Anglia regiment, but they have retained a regimental museum at The Keep, Gibraltar Barracks, Newmarket Road, Bury St Edmunds.

The Fall of Singapore
As Peter so ably recalls in his memoir, his Battalion arrived in Singapore when it was in a state of chaos. The Japanese were

already advancing down the Malay Peninsula and many of the Europeans realized that they would have to get out if they were not to be captured by the Japanese.

Singapore was supposed to be an impregnable fortress. It was the key to British possessions in the Far East and had, in the 1930s, been heavily fortified. The British believed that their powerful fortress would show the Japanese that they were invincible.

Malaya was first attacked soon after Pearl Harbour. On 9 December 1941, the city was bombed and almost all front line planes were lost during the attack. This destroyed any chance of aerial support for the army during the attack on Malaya and then Singapore.

The British believed that the strength of their navy would deter the Japanese. The base contained a squadron of warships led by the modern battleship the *Prince of Wales* and the battle cruiser *Repulse*. On 10 December both these ships were sunk after attacks by Japanese torpedo bombers. There was no RAF protection for the battleships.

The Malayan mainland was invaded by the Japanese Twenty-Fifth army on 8 December 1941. They arrived by amphibious assault from Indochina. Now the army led by Lieutenant General Arthur Percival stood alone against the Japanese. Comprising 90,000 men, it was a mix of British, Australian and Indian troops. Facing him was General Tomoyuki Yamashita. Many of his troops were battle hardened after campaigns in Manchuria and China.

The troops engaged at the Battle of Jitra (11–12 December 1941) and the British, Australians and Indians were soundly beaten. The Japanese pushed south through the peninsula – speed was their greatest weapon. Often using bicycles they sped through the jungle and frequently outflanked the Allied troops, giving them no time to regroup.

The Japanese had been ordered to take no prisoners – it was thought they would slow up the advance. Wounded allied prisoners were killed as soon as they were captured, and some of the able-bodied who surrendered were also killed. Some Australian troops were doused with petrol and then set alight. Local Malays or Chinese who helped the Allies were tortured and murdered.

On 11 January the Japanese had taken Kuala Lumpar and by 31 January the British, Australian and Indian forces had withdrawn across the Johor Strait. The causeway between Singapore Island and

181

the mainland was destroyed. Peter Jackson arrived in Singapore on 16 January at a time when the evacuation was beginning, and there were still hopes the island could be held.

The Japanese attack started on 8 February. At this stage the Japanese had only 23,000 troops, far less than the 100,000 commanded by General Percival, but he had spread his troops too thinly and the Japanese broke through. One such area was on the Woodlands Road near where Peter was stationed.

Within a week Singapore was in the hands of the Japanese. The official surrender was on 15 February 1942 – the day of Chinese New Year. About 80,000 men were taken prisoner to join the 50,000 already captured by the Japanese in Malaya. Those who surrendered in Singapore included 32,000 Indians, 16,000 British and 14,000 Australians. It was the worst military defeat in British or Australian history.

When Peter was captured he had a First World War Lee-Enfield rifle and five rounds of ammunition. He had been directed to defend a strong point with his team of Australians.

Many of those captured in Singapore were imprisoned at Changi and were, like Peter, often deployed as work gangs in the city. Others were shipped in prisoner transports, known as 'hellships' to work in other parts of Asia, particularly Japan.

The Indians, as Peter discovered, often joined the 'Indian National Army' and they fought the British in Burma; others became prisoner guards at Changi. Probably about 30,000 of them did this. Others who remained loyal to the British were shipped off to work as forced labour in the Pacific.

Changi Prison
Changi prison was built by the British in 1936 and, following the fall of Singapore, 3,000 civilians were detained here in a space designed for 600. Most of the captured Allied soldiers, about 50,000 of them, were housed in the British army's Selarang Barracks – most of these were British or Australian soldiers. When the troops arrived the complex had been badly damaged by the fighting and there was no running water and no sanitation. Peter remembers little about any time spent there as he soon 'volunteered' for work in Singapore.

Although the Allied troops were housed on various parts of the island, Changi has become the general name used by those prisoners who were close to the original British jail.

182

Only about 858 POWs died at Changi although many more, who were transported from here to the Thai-Burma Death Railway or the Sandakan airfield in Borneo, died there.

In 1944 Allied POWs, largely Australians built a chapel at the prison. They used simple tools and what materials they could find. A British airman, Stanley Warren, painted a series of murals at the chapel.

After the war the chapel was dismantled and shipped to Australia and in 1988 it was reconstructed and re-assembled at the Royal Military College Duntroon, near Canberra.

The Thai-Burma Railway

After working for the Japanese in Singapore, Peter, like most other Allied POWs who remained in Singapore and were in reasonable physical condition, were sent north to the jungles of Thailand. Here he was to work on the 415km stretch of railway running from Ban Pong (Thailand) to Thanbyuzayat (Burma). The Japanese wanted to construct the railway so that they could shift supplies to their troops fighting the British in Burma – their sea route through the Straits of Malacca was vulnerable to allied air attack. The British had already considered building this railway at the beginning of the twentieth century, but felt that the proposed route through hilly, heavily forested terrain crossed by countless rivers was too difficult to complete.

Work on the railway started in June 1942. The journey for many was as Peter describes it. The conditions on the trains were horrific and they were crowded into every available space. As they moved up the railway Peter was able to see some of the work that had already been completed, so it is probable he did not leave Singapore until early in 1943. He, like most of the other prisoners, was forced to march from the railhead, often for five or six days until they reached their camp. The camps were sited at fifteen-mile intervals along the rail track.

About 60,000 Allied prisoners of war were used on the construction of the railway. Alongside them worked another 180,000 Asian labourers. About 16,000 Allied personnel died as a result of work on the railway, as did 90,000 Asians.

Peter believes that he was probably taken to the Songkrai II camp, although he cannot confirm that. But given his description of the trip there he was probably somewhere near the Three Pagoda Pass. It is thought that nearly 3,000 POWs died in its vicinity.

One of the first jobs of those who arrived at the new camps was to build the huts for guards and then for themselves. Cooking sheds and the inevitable hospital also had to be built. Some of this was work that Peter did. He was responsible for laying paths for the Japanese and digging their latrines.

The methods used to build the railway were very primitive. Much of the work of cutting the track through the jungle was done by hand. Sticks were placed to show the level of the track and gangs of prisoners had to grub out the earth beside the track with a primitive hoe-like implement called a *chunkel*. There was little mechanical equipment used. Much of the material, including sleepers and rails, used in the construction of the railway came from lines that were dismantled in Malaya or even the Dutch East Indies. In their hurry the Japanese often sourced green timber for some of the bridges and embankments. In time these shrunk and created the need for further maintenance.

The Japanese were in a hurry to get the railway completed and so the methods they used and the demands they made on the prisoners were crippling and were responsible for many deaths. Water-borne diseases like cholera were deadly, and it was an epidemic of this in the camp, where Peter was stationed, that gave them the opportunity to escape.

By 17 October 1943 the two sections of the railway met about 18km south of the Three Pagoda Pass. Those POWs who were still fit enough to work were then transferred to Japan or other parts of their empire. Those who were left were responsible for maintaining the railway and suffered terribly from privation. Others were confined in hospital camps where there was little food. Some were killed in Allied Air attacks. POWs were forced to repair the bridges blown up, but by June 1945 the railway had been so badly bombed that it was no longer useable.

What saved many Allied POW lives was the underground operation organized by Peter Heath, Boon Pong and many other sympathetic Thais. They managed to smuggle money, medicines and sometimes additional food into the camps. Known as the V-Scheme, those who operated it or knew of its existence were extraordinarily brave as the Japanese would have tortured and killed anyone whom they found was involved. Regretfully such assistance was not available to those like Peter who were imprisoned. He and his mates were incredibly lucky to survive.

The Escape

Peter and six others escaped from the camp on 6 June 1943. Their treatment, fear that they would succumb to cholera and the opportunity offered by the number of sick Japanese guards allowed them to get away. They moved quickly away from the route of the railway into some rough and very isolated country and many of the villages were deserted.

He believes the escape was organized by Sergeant Ian Bradley. His younger brother Corporal Bernard Bradley was also with the group. Bernard Bradley survived but Ian died in Changi shortly after being released from Outram Road Prison. Others were James Hedley, a Singapore resident and member of the Singapore Volunteer Army Reserve. He was able to speak Malay and Thai and this was a great help to them. Sergeant Jimmy Singleton died of suspected cholera in the Cave where the party lived for four months before they were finally betrayed by the Burmese. Peter thinks that the cave was the Jimbat Cave and is probably a well-known local feature.

The other three were Fred (no surname) who was a London Cockney and who was always good for a laugh, Joe Dawkins a Londoner who survived, as did Taffy Ellis a Welsh Corporal.

Peter said, 'We were a close-knit group and our one aim was to survive the horrors that we had seen. We never argued even when we let the goat live – that really tested our relationship. All in all we were a great bunch of mates.'

Even today Peter still feels very sad when he mentions the death of Jimmy so far away from his own home in the depths of the jungle. But it was his death that saved them. The Japanese were particularly cruel to those who escaped. Torture followed by death was usually the fate of those who organized escapes and the fact that the men were able to blame Jimmy for the escape meant that some survived to be freed by the Allies

Peter is not sure what happened to the group. Once they were recaptured they were usually forbidden to talk to one another and after their trial they were divided up and so contact was lost.

Moulmain (now Mawlamyaing)

Peter, now a prisoner, arrived at Moulmain by river. The town had a long association with the British and became the first capital of British Burma in 1826. Peter saw nothing of the town and its famous pagoda, but even then the words of Kipling's famous poem, Mandalay rang in his head:

> By the old Moulmein Pagoda, lookin' lazy at the sea, There's a Burma girl a-settin', and I know she thinks o' me; For the wind is in the palm-trees, and the temple-bells they say;
>
> > Come you back, you British Soldier;
> > come you back to Mandalay!

Outram Road Prison, Singapore

Peter was moved from Moulmain to Bangkok, where he and the others with whom he escaped were tried. They were then moved to Singapore and the Outram Road Prison, the main prison for all those whom the Japanese felt had in some way broken the rules they imposed. Allied prisoners of war who, like Peter Jackson, escaped, ended up there. At first many of the prisoners were in solitary confinement but when the numbers increased they were housed two to a cell. Peter's experiences capture so much of the horror of those who suffered imprisonment there. But as his memoir tells, he survived and was repatriated to Britain towards the end of 1945.

Coming to New Zealand, 1952

Peter said:

> It was a typically cold, wet London Monday morning and I was on my way to work on the London underground, when I noticed a new advertisement. It was of man sitting on a horse looking over acres of green fields. He was shading his eyes from the hot sun. In the distance was a large mob of sheep; in the foreground some grazing cows. Beneath in large letters were the words 'Buy New Zealand butter and lamb'. The whole sign really cheered me up and I couldn't stop thinking about it all day.
>
> In the evening Margaret, my wife, told me she had heard a very interesting radio talk on New Zealand. She added there was going to be a talk in a hotel about the country and she had noted the time and the date. I have always taken notice of coincidences and this was too good to ignore.

186

We attended the meeting and afterwards the speaker said that if anyone was interested in migrating there he would be pleased to interview them. He said that New Zealand was looking for skilled tradesmen particularly in the building trade.

When my turn came the interviewer asked me a number of questions and then said, 'I suppose you were in the army?'

'Oh Yes! I had no choice; I was a conscript.' He then told me that he had been in the army so we started to swap stories.

Suddenly he stopped. 'We got a bit carried away there. Could you build a house if we put four pegs on the side of a hill?'

'Probably – anyhow I'd have a jolly good try.'

'Peter! You're in!'

Not long after a I received a letter from Fletcher Construction company in Auckland asking me if I was prepared to work for them. I wrote back immediately and said, 'Yes!'

Finally a year after I made the initial application we all finished up in Christchurch. I worked for Fletchers for twelve and a half years and then joined a private firm where I stayed until I retired.

I have never regretted coming to New Zealand.

As a Postscript to his story Peter wrote:

I was happy in civilian life
Not too much worry, not too much strife
Until one day into the army you must go
I was never given the chance to say 'No!'

Hither and thither, here and yon,
Through no fault of my own have I gone,
Good times and bad times, sometime sad
O God how I missed my wife, Mum and Dad.

They sent me out East, it wasn't the best
But I thank the Almighty I didn't go West.

So I've been able to write my story,
Not too much blood, not too much glory,
But at least it's true, not any lies,
It's the way I saw it while I was there.

Peter Jackson

Note on language

I have not altered the Japanese language that is in the text. This is because it is the soldiers' language. As Peter said, 'It is what I picked up by ear while I was a prisoner and I never saw it written.' I decided to leave his transcriptions, because it is a memoir and it is what he learned to use.

Lack of Photos

It is impossible to get images that record Peter's experience in Singapore, Malaya and Thailand. He did not have a camera and if any of men had been seen using one they would have been executed immediately. There are at least five artists who risked their lives to paint scenes of the Burma-Thai Death Railway: Jack Bridger Chalker, Ronald Searle, Murray Griffin, Ashley Old and Philip Meninsky. Much of their work is either in Australia or at the Imperial War Museum in London.

All of them risked death if they had been caught making drawings. Ronald Searle hid his under the mattresses of those prisoners who were dying of cholera. Others hid them in the walls of their huts or buried them. All prisoners were denied access to any pencils or paper so that those who made these drawings were very resourceful and brave.